D0073263

Theology and political society

Theology and political society

THE HULSEAN LECTURES IN
THE UNIVERSITY OF CAMBRIDGE
1978

CHARLES DAVIS

WAGGONER LIBRARY
DISCARD

CAMBRIDGE UNIVERSITY PRESS
Cambridge
London   New York   New Rochelle
Melbourne   Sydney

MACKEY LIBRARY
TREVECCA NAZARENE COLLEGE

Published by the Press Syndicate of the University of Cambridge
The Pitt Building, Trumpington Street, Cambridge CB2 1RP
32 East 57th Street, New York, NY 10022, USA
296 Beaconsfield Parade, Middle Park, Melbourne 3206, Australia

© Cambridge University Press 1980

First published 1980

Photoset, printed and bound
in Great Britain by
REDWOOD BURN LIMITED
Trowbridge & Esher

British Library Cataloguing in Publication Data

Davis, Charles
    Theology and political society. – (Hulsean lectures; 1978).
    1. Christianity and politics
    I. Title   II. Series
    261.7   BR115.P7   80–40014

    ISBN 0 521 22538 8

FOR ANTHONY

Contents

Preface

Most of the preparatory work for this book was done during a sabbatical leave, 1976–7, at Cambridge University. I have to thank the Rector and administration of Concordia University for granting the leave and also the Canada Council (now the Social Sciences and Humanities Research Council of Canada) for its grant of a Leave Fellowship. My thanks are also due to Clare Hall for electing me to a Visiting Fellowship and providing me with an excellent environment for study. It was during the sabbatical leave that I was chosen as Hulsean Lecturer for 1977–8, an honour which I deeply appreciate. I am indeed most grateful to the Faculty of Divinity at Cambridge, especially Professors Geoffrey Lampe and Donald McKinnon, for the way they made me welcome during my leave and invited me to participate in the seminars and other activities of the Faculty. That same welcome was shown me when I returned in April 1978 to deliver the lectures. I owe especial thanks to Dr McKinnon, then the Norris-Hulse Professor, who acted as my host, and to Dr Nicholas Lash, his successor in that Chair, who reinforced his welcome. For the period of the lectures, I stayed at St Edmund's House, and I want to thank the Master, John Coventry, the Dean, Christopher Ryan, the Fellows and the resident students for a comfortable, enjoyable and stimulating visit.

Department of Religion　　　　　　　　　　　　　　　　　　C.D.
Concordia University
Montreal, Canada

ix

1

From orthodoxy to politics

The Second Vatican Council came to an end on 8 December 1965. Everyone at the time saw the Council as a new beginning. Some were disappointed at the hesitations and compromises that in their opinion had marred the Council documents. Others were afraid that the clarity of Church teaching had been obscured by a dangerous dalliance with modern ideas. But both progressives and conservatives understood the Council as marking out the future for Catholic theology and action, whether as a salient to be pushed further or as a line to be defended. People were for that reason bewildered when in a year or two it began to be apparent that the Council was not an opening to the future, but the closing of the books on a past era. Vatican Two did not turn out to be another Trent. Trent had dominated the Catholic scene for centuries, so that theology became little more than a commentary on its declarations and Catholic practice the putting into effect of its decrees. The documents of the Second Vatican Council are already now chiefly of interest to the historian. They are of little or no use to the theologian in tackling the present issues of theology and of even less help in the pressing questions of Catholic practice.

What at first created a false impression was the gap that before the Council had separated Roman theology from the Catholic theology current in France and Germany. During its four sessions from 1962 to 1965, the Council provided the Catholic hierarchy of the world, mostly trained in Rome, with a rapid updating of their theology, showing them that Catholic theology was not confined to the unalterable concepts of the Roman classicist mentality.[1]

The majority of the bishops found the new theology accept-

1

able, so that after the Council it was no longer credible to suggest that theologians like Congar, de Lubac, Chenu, Schillebeeckx or Rahner were undermining the true faith. In the sense of a catching-up with Catholic theology itself the Council was an *aggiornamento* for the bishops and the rest of the Church. But the theology thus hurriedly and somewhat incoherently assimilated had already run its course.

That theology, which blazed forth at Vatican Two only to die away, may be characterized as orthodoxy transposed into an anthropocentric mode. It was orthodox doctrine interpreted in transcendentalist, existentialist and personalist terms. It was a theology centred upon man, a theology expressive of an 'integral humanism' – to use Jacques Maritain's phrase, taken up by Paul VI.[2] Orthodox and anthropocentric: both these characteristics now disqualify the theology of Vatican renewal. Immediately after the Council theology entered the present era in which – if certain insights are consistently maintained – orthodoxy in the usual sense of that word is impossible in fact and inappropriate as an ideal and in which there is no place for man as such, because man as such is an abstraction.

Orthodoxy makes doctrine a final norm and thus implies the primacy of theory over practice. Such primacy is the very definition of ideology as false consciousness, which must be cleansed by establishing the primacy of practice. Humanism in its career from the Renaissance to existentialism exalted Man with a capital M. This was in effect to evade social reality with an abstraction. Human reality as the object of genuine knowledge is men and women in groups – social classes, national or linguistic communities, historical generations (Fierro, 1977: 84). Man as such is not a reality but a mental idol. Theology that has assimilated those two insights must be practical and critical, not dominated by theory in the shape of orthodox doctrine nor by ideological abstractions such as man or human nature – let alone supernature.

There has, then, been a break of some magnitude in the tradition of theology. We may describe this break as the move to 'political theology' – provided we understand that phrase in a particular way. 'Political theology' in the sense intended does not mean the theology of politics, namely theological reflection having politics as its object. It is not, in other words, another regional theology, alongside theologies such as the theology of work, the theology of terrestrial realities, the theology of history, the theology of religions and so on. The proliferation of such regional theologies belongs to the humanist stage of traditional theology, when Christian doctrine was applied to a variety of human problems. Political theology as understood here is a new style of theology, a new way of doing theology, a new method or dimension that affects theology as a whole. It is not a part of theology, but theology in its entirety done politically.

Every theology is faith as mediated[3] by some cultural element. (The same may be said of beliefs in so far as these are distinct from faith, but that must come later.) In other words, theology is a product of the interaction between faith and some element in the cultural matrix of faith. Different types of theology are mediated by different kinds of cultural elements. Consequently, a break in the continuity of theology occurs whenever there is a change in the cultural element that serves to mediate it. Scholastic theology was mediated by metaphysics, positive theology by textual exegesis and historiography, transcendentalist, existentialist and personalist theologies by modern forms of humanism. Political theology is theology mediated by the political. It is faith as articulated or brought to expression in and through political practice. Just as there is no straight-line development between Scholastic theology and positive theology nor between positive theology and existentialist theology, so too political theology is not a straight-line continuation of preceding theologies. 'Political theology', writes Fierro, 'is a distinct theology, a new and original theology that makes a break with all those theologies that have gone before' (1977: 44).

What sets political theology over against all earlier theologies and further seems to put it into conflict with the continuity of Christian tradition itself is its acceptance of the Marxist concept of critique. Marx rejected the concept of theory as immune from practice and its variations. He refused the claim of theoretical thought to be a presuppositionless, contemplative recognition of a stable object. Theory and practice are interdependent, and theoretical activity, like the practical activity with which it is one, is a product of the changing reality of society. This new understanding of the relation between theory and practice implied the abolition of philosophy as traditionally understood and its sublation or transformation into critique, namely into critical thought as the conscious component of social practice. The new concept of critique is expressed briefly and forcibly in the *Theses on Feuerbach*. The eleventh thesis is so well known as hardly to bear repetition: 'The philosophers have only *interpreted* the world, in various ways; the point is to *change* it' (Colletti, ed., 1975: 423 – Marx's italics). It is, however, the second thesis that states the epistemological point most explicitly: 'The question whether objective truth can be attributed to human thinking is not a question of theory but is a *practical* question. Man must prove the truth, i.e. the reality and power, the this-sidedness of his thinking practice. The dispute over the reality or non-reality of thinking that is isolated from practice is a purely scholastic question' (*ibid.*, 422 – Marx's italics).

There are those, and the advocates of political theology are among them, who consider that Marx's concept of the unity of theory and practice is a turning-point in the history of Western thought, dividing critical thought when self-consciously dependent upon social practice from all previous forms of theoretical reflection. In the same way the introduction into theology of the principle of critique with its relation to social practice is seen as distinguishing political theology from all previous theologies. Orthodoxy is correspondingly transformed into *orthopraxis*.[4]

Some of the political theologies may be briefly reviewed here from that standpoint.

Johann Baptist Metz, the inaugurator of political theology in its German form, has himself indicated the new theory–practice relationship as the key factor in its emergence. In his brief article on political theology in the encyclopaedia *Sacramentum Mundi* he expresses the matter succinctly: 'Political theology claims to be a basic element in the whole structure of critical theological thinking, motivated by a new notion of the relation between theory and practice, according to which all theology must be of itself "practical", orientated to action' (1970a: 47 n. 3). All the same, that statement is not so strong as might have been expected. To speak of theology as 'oriented to action' hardly marks a fundamental change in theological method. The context, with its reference to the new theory–practice dialectic, requires 'mediated by social practice' or something similar. Is Metz's appeal to the unity of theory and practice fully consistent? Two of his former students, Xhaufflaire (1972: 117–42) and van den Oudenrijn (1972: 209–17), have questioned the consistency of Metz's theology on this point, and they themselves have offered a much more thorough-going application of the Marxian concept of *praxis* to theology (Xhaufflaire and Derksen, 1970: 303–83; van den Oudenrijn, 1972).

Metz, however, has continued his reflections. In his most recent statement, *Glaube in Geschichte und Gesellschaft* (1977a), he admits that the writings of his students – he mentions Xhaufflaire and van den Oudenrijn – alerted him to the limits of a purely theoretical 'critical theology'. The starting-point of political theology was, he reaffirms, the primacy of practice, so that for it the basic problem of theology became, not the relation between dogma and history, but the relation between faith and social practice. But he goes on to acknowledge that his earlier formulations were defective and the political expression of his theology too often confined to exhortation. The explanation he offers is that he leant too heavily upon Kant and Kant's primacy of the practical reason and did not sufficiently advert to the difference between Kant and Marx (1977a: 47–51). Ethical practice he now sees is not socially innocent or politically neutral. Kant was able to summon people to become adults and shake off their self-imposed tutelage, because he was addressing those who were socially and economically in possession of power. But there is a socially imposed immaturity of the poor and oppressed. Christian practice has to concern itself above all with those who are prevented by social conditions from becoming fully mature as human subjects. For that reason Christian practice cannot be merely ethical, but must also be social and political. Metz now gives such prominence to the struggle to enable all men to become subjects that he characterizes political theology in general as a political theology of the subject. He presents God as a practical idea: that is, the thought of God is what prevents the ideal that all men be freed to become fully human subjects

5

from being a mere utopian projection and instead sustains it as a serious option.

The question here, however, is not so much the nature of Christian practice, but the primacy of practice. How Metz now understands that primacy can be gathered better from his recent work on the following of Christ (1977b). There he conceives Christology as a practical knowledge. Christ is the way. Every attempt to know him or to understand him must be a following of him. Only by following him do we know with whom we are dealing. The following of Christ is not therefore a subsequent application of Christology. To suppose so would be to confuse the Logos of Christian faith with the Logos of the Greeks. Christ must be so thought that he is never merely thought. Christology does not simply instruct us in our following of Christ; it draws upon the practice of following Christ for its own very truth. It is essentially a practical knowledge. In that sense, so Metz argues, every Christology stands under the primacy of practice. He therefore claims that the dialectic of Christology, which is a dialectic of the following of Christ, is not a conceptual dialectic of an idealist kind, but a theory–practice dialectic that takes account of Marx and the post-idealist problematic (1977b: 41–2).

I must confess that here Metz does not convince me. He has, in my opinion, turned aside from the insight that religious teaching like other forms of theory is entirely mediated through social practice. It will not serve to say that the following of Christ mediates a Christology, which is thus a practical knowledge. If one consistently holds to the theory–practice dialectic, the practice that fundamentally has to mediate Christian faith cannot itself be already specifically Christian as a product of Christian faith. For the basic derivation of Christian faith we must go back to the qualities of social practice as human action. Since the Christian message is a message of liberation, what mediates it is social practice as directed towards human emancipation. Or, to put it in another way, Christian faith is grounded when emancipatory social action brings us to the limits of human meaning, so that we experience in Christ a transcendent source of hope and liberation. The mediation of emancipatory social action does not deny God's initiative or gift, but simply indicates the context and means through which his action comes to us. It does not come to us as a theoretical message, which we must then put into practice, but only in and through our own human social action as directed to the liberation of all and to the establishment of a human community in freedom.

Metz, however, as Bauer has pointed out (1976: 221), will not allow that the truth of Christianity, eschatological in nature as it is, is socially and politically mediated in its entirety. He rejects the Marxian total mediation of theory through practice and places himself with Kant as holding to the non-identity of theory and practice. At the centre of the Christian faith, Metz declares, is the memory of the crucified Lord, a particular remembrance of suffering, which grounds the promise of future freedom for all. That is an eschatological statement, which cannot be completely verified or established; it remains open to contention (Metz, 1972a: 127). Bauer (1976: 221) elucidates the matter with a reference to Sölle. She writes: 'political theology, however, grounds its understanding of truth in the still undisclosed unity of theory and praxis. From the gospel it obtains the nonderivable promise . . . the verification principle of every theological statement is the praxis that it enables for the future' (1974: 76).

Wiedenhofer, consequently, distinguishes (1976: 20–3) two phases in the development of German political theology, particularly that of Metz. In the first phase political theology took over the critique of ideology and accepted the new relationship of theory and practice. That resulted in a new understanding of the task and method of theology. But what marks the second phase is a concern to establish the specifically Christian and theological character of political theology.

Metz himself has drawn his political theology back within the traditional Christian orbit by formulating what is briefly called his 'Memoria-thesis' (1972a; 1977a: 87–103). In effect, rather than following the path taken by some of his students and stressing the function of practice, Metz has instead revised the concept of theory, so as to place it within a Christian context. Theory is now understood as *Erinnerung* (remembrance), namely, in the concrete as the memory of suffering. He sees the memory of human suffering as resulting in a new understanding of history and of political action. First,

7

the suffering of men stands opposed to any affirmative theory of reconciliation between man and nature and therefore to any idea that the substratum of history is nature conceived as development or process. History as the history of suffering has no goal, only a future. Eschatology thus excludes teleology in the understanding of history. Second, the remembered history of suffering leads to a new concept of political action. The memory of suffering takes on the form of a 'dangerous memory' or 'subversive tradition'. It forces us politically to view public affairs, not from the standpoint of the successful and the well-established, but from that of the conquered and the victims. The working of the memory of suffering as a subversive tradition is essentially practical in nature. But with it, the concept of *praxis* is widened. *Praxis* is now not only action, but also suffering. It keeps its social and historical character, but, since it now includes the whole of human suffering, the concern is not just with social oppression, but with the whole gamut of human distress before guilt, finitude and death.

Once political life and action are conceived as arising out of the memory of human suffering taken in its widest range, the way becomes open, Metz argues, for a contribution from the great moral and religious traditions. For Christians, the sufferings and death of Christ become a dangerous memory, giving the lie to the affirmative teleology of modern evolutionary consciousness and also placing them on the side of the victims of history, instead of on that of the victors. The Christian tradition is thus understood as a subversive tradition, the working of which is 'essentially practical in nature' (Metz, 1972a: 126). For tradition to work in a practical fashion is not the same as for practice to mediate tradition. With all his repeated stress on practice, Metz seems to me constantly to evade the chief bearing of the unity of theory and practice, namely that the body of teaching constituting tradition cannot be disengaged from the changing reality of social practice. It cannot be placed apart as an independent whole, which is then applicable 'in practice' to every historical situation. Theory, or in this instance traditional symbols and doctrines, are part of social history, constituting the conscious component of a particular social practice. There is a unity and continuity of social practice, and so there is a unity and continuity of theory, but, just as the past social practice of Christians is open to criticism in the light of the goal of human liberation, so in the same measure does the Christian tradition require a careful assessment to discriminate the residue of oppression from the product of the movement to emancipation. According to the theory–practice dialectic, there is no purely theoretical centre of reference for the truth and continuing identity of tradition. As the conscious component of social practice, its past and present meaning and truth as lying beyond all ideological distortion and mystification can be assessed only in the social practice to which it has always been essentially related. Since the identity and truth of a tradition cannot be established theoretically, the religious structure we refer to as orthodoxy is rendered impossible. Orthodoxy treats doctrine, not practice, as the final norm; it therefore presupposes a contemplative concept of truth, which disengages it from practice.

Metz's half-hearted and inconsistent acceptance of the primacy of practice comes out clearly in an article dealing with *orthopraxis*. He sees *orthopraxis*, not as replacing orthodoxy, but as the price of orthodoxy. In other words, orthodoxy, presented as the liberation of the populace from its ignorance and superstition, is a desirable state only to be won for the Christian people through or at the cost of diligent *orthopraxis* (1974; reproduced in a revised version in Metz, 1977a: 120–35). Here, on the one hand, practice leads to doctrine or theory, but, on the other hand, it is not a question of mediating doctrinal insights, but of drawing the populace into a pre-existing doctrinal structure, namely orthodoxy. The new language covers a traditional outlook.

All this shows how the mainline theological tradition has reasserted itself in German political theology, so that there has been a drawing back from the more revolutionary implications of its original insights. It is still true, however, that the discontinuity, the break, the newness of political theology lies primarily in the attempt to assimilate into Christian thinking the dialectic of theory and practice, even though it has not been carried through consistently.

When we turn from German political theology to that other version, known as the theology of liberation, which has come to us from Latin America, we find a clear recognition of the

Marxist heritage, particularly the primacy of practice (Gutiérrez, 1973: 9–10). Despite the paucity of methodological
discussions, no one can doubt that behind Latin American
theology lies an acute consciousness that the doing of Christian truth in social and political action must take precedence
over any theoretical statement or interpretations. Political
theology is 'nothing else but the thoughts produced by faith
on the humus of Marxism'. The remark is from Alfredo Fierro
(1977: 80), a Spaniard, who from Madrid gives an analysis of
contemporary political theologies, both Latin American and
German. He gives the most forcible expression I have met with
of the turn of theology towards *praxis*, the break with earlier
theologies and the impossibility of orthodoxy (*ibid.*, 21–2).

Fierro makes an observation that places the stress of political
theology upon practice in a wider context. 'This thesis', he
writes, 'that knowledge originates in praxis, cannot be considered specifically Marxist today, however. It is imbedded in the
deepest presuppositions of present-day science and culture,
because it represents a configuration of Western thinking that
goes back to the Enlightenment. Introduced into more
modern Western thought by Marx, it is now a common heritage rather than the private property of Marxism' (*ibid.*, 90).
Which means that with political theology we are confronted
with the latest phase in the long dialogue between Christian
faith and modern reason. The question now is not the relation
between science and revelation or between dogma and historical knowledge, but between faith and social practice. Theology in such a context has to find a place as a form of critical
reflection upon practice, as critique when carried out under
the horizon of faith.

The break of political theology with earlier theology,
centred as that was upon a contemplative interpretation of
prior symbols, texts and doctrines, is also found in two forms
of liberation theology produced in North America: feminist
theology and black theology.

Mary Daly in *Beyond God the Father* contrasts her approach
with any theology 'which supposes some unique and change-
less revelation peculiar to Christianity or to *any* religion' (1973:
7 – Daly's italics). Such a theology she sees exemplified in the
work of Karl Barth, 'which implicitly holds as sacred the pre-

suppositions of patriarchy' (*ibid.*, 200 n. 8). Daly is not interested in applying existing doctrines to women's liberation in the traditional theological manner, but is concerned to promote the emerging awareness and creativity of women. This excludes conforming to any preconceived pattern. When the positive products of women's liberation 'express dimensions of the search for ultimate meaning, they can indeed be called both philosophical and theological, but in the sense of pointing beyond the God of patriarchal philosophy and religion' (*ibid.*, 7). What therefore comes first in feminist theology is not doctrine or theory, but women's experience and action, through which new philosophical and theological meaning will be mediated.

When James Cone speaks of the sources and norm of black theology, he calls revelation '*a black event, i.e.*, what black people are doing about their liberation' (1970: 65 – Cone's italics). The first three theological sources he lists are black experience, black history and black culture. He goes on to give a place to Scripture and tradition, but says pointedly: 'Black Theology is only concerned with that tradition of Christianity which is usable in the black liberation struggle. As it looks over the past, it asks: "How is the Christian tradition related to the oppression of black people in America?"' (*ibid.*, 74).

The book abounds in extreme expressions. For example: 'Black Theology refuses to accept a God who is not identified totally with the goals of the black community. If God is not for us and against white people, then he is a murderer and we had better kill him' (*ibid.*, 59–60). But as Juan Segundo remarks: 'Cone's book is a much more serious theological effort than many people might think at first glance' (1977: 25). Its advantage for my present purpose is that it illustrates vividly the magnitude of the shift involved when theology is not conceived as theoretical reflection upon permanent doctrines, but as the critical consciousness of Christian social practice – something that is apt to be lost sight of in the convolutions of German theological discourse.

The change in theological outlook signalled by the emergence of political theology, including the theologies of liberation, has its counterpart in the general mentality of Christians. The change is particularly noticeable among

11

Catholics. There has been a loss of trust in spiritual ideas and doctrines as such and a growing indifference towards traditional orthodox dogmas among those active in their faith. Hence the bewilderment of others at what has happened, as for example of the writer in *The Clergy Review*, who found in talking to seminarians, priests, sisters, theologians, intellectuals, all Catholic in some official sense, that there was no way of telling in advance whether the person held any of the dogmatic or moral views once considered as making one identifiably Catholic (Schall, 1977: 261). And a succession of writers have expressed their dismay and anger at finding that the post-conciliar epoch for the Catholic Church did not bring an orderly acceptance of Council teaching, but the apparent cessation of the authority of the whole of the previous dogmatic tradition.

For those not prepared to dismiss the changed outlook as simply a loss of faith, political theology may be seen as an attempt, with the use of the Marxian dialectic of theory and practice, to give systematic expression to the conviction that the identity and truth of the Christian faith can no longer be maintained by doctrinal assertion or theoretical interpretation, but only by the experience of that identity and truth as mediated in and through a social practice of liberation. As Segundo puts it in his comments upon Cone: 'orthodoxy possesses no ultimate criterion in itself because being orthodox does not mean possessing the final truth. We only arrive at the latter by orthopraxis. It is the latter that is the ultimate criterion of the former, both in theology and in biblical interpretation. The truth is truth only when it serves as the basis for truly human attitudes' (1977: 32).

The turn of theology away from orthodoxy towards politics took place in the middle of the sixties. Here are a few key dates:

The end of the Second Vatican Council in 1965, which all unknowingly cleared the decks for a new and most unexpected post-conciliar era in the Catholic Church, was followed among Protestants by the World Conference on Church and Society, organized by the World Council of Churches in July 1967 in Geneva, which, in a manner disturbing to many Christians, insisted forthrightly on the involvement of the

Churches in radical social action. The Conference stimulated theological reflection united to social action.

Metz first put forward the name and concept of political theology in a symposium held in Chicago in March 1966 (Burke, 1966 – republished in Metz, 1973a: 81–97), and then presented his ideas in more detail in a paper read at the Congress on the Theology of the Renewal of the Church, held in Toronto as part of the Canadian Centenary in 1967 (Shook, ed., II, 1968 – republished in Metz, 1973a: 107–30).

Earlier, in 1964, Moltmann, who with Metz drew inspiration for his theology from the thought of Ernst Bloch and who quickly followed Metz in speaking of political theology, had published in German his *Theology of Hope*. In subsequent writings, Moltmann applied his theology of hope to political life with the help of the theology of the cross, but in doing so he has simply extended its original meaning. Douglas Meeks is able to say that Moltmann's political theology is 'the core' of his theology of hope (1974: 129). Although their theologies remain distinctive, Moltmann and Metz are co-representatives of German political theology and have collaborated in promoting its basic aims.

On a more popular but influential level, Harvey Cox's *Secular City* appeared in 1965.

In 1968 took place the famous Medellín Conference, namely the Second General Conference of Latin American Bishops (CELAM II), held at Medellín, Colombia. Despite some weaknesses and lacunae in its work, the Conference was a major event for the Church in Latin America. 'At Medellín', writes Gutiérrez, 'the Latin American Church, despite the climate created by the Eucharistic Congress held in Bogota immediately before it, realistically perceived the world in which it was and clearly saw its place in that world' (1973: 134). Gary MacEoin, quoting its statements, sums up what the Conference did in these words:

CELAM II opted positively for the poor, the voiceless, the oppressed. It identified the source of oppression as institutionalized violence, the neocolonialism of the national oligarchies, and the external neocolonialism of 'the international monopolies and the international imperialism of money'; a situation calling for 'global, caring, urgent and basically renewing change'. The commitment to radical transformation was unambiguous: 'a thirst for complete emancipation, liberation from every subjection, personal growth and social solidarity' (MacEoin, 1978b: 1–2).[5]

The impulse of the Conference helped to produce the theology of liberation found in the writings of Gutiérrez, Segundo, Assman and Alves from 1968 onwards.

This would seem to be the place to make a distinction between German political theology and the Latin American theology of liberation. I have followed the usage of Fierro in including them both under the title of political theology, because, whatever their differences, they act, as he says, in a parallel way 'as creators of a new theological space' (1977: 18). Nevertheless, they remain, as Fiorenza makes clear, 'distinctly different attempts to work out the relation between faith and praxis, religion and society' (1975: 5). I will follow here Fiorenza's comparative analysis, which contrasts the two approaches under three points.

First, each theology gives a different reading of secularization. For the Germans the modern world is secularized as having cast off the tutelage of religion, so that a sense of the absence of God pervades modern culture. While political theology gives a positive interpretation of modernity, welcoming the freedom and pluralism it has brought and seeing it as a challenge to rethink the experience of transcendence, it vigorously opposes one of its effects, namely the privatization of faith, which means the relegation of faith to the private, individual sphere, and it is critical of the so-called theology of secularization for having reinforced that exclusion of faith from the public sphere. The Latin American theologians on their part accuse the German theologians of giving universality to the particular cultural situation of Western Europe. Latin America is not marked by an exclusion of religion from public life. The Church is not absent from culture and politics, but is intimately involved with society, though only too often in support of established governments. Secularization is indeed reaching Latin America, but it will have an historical unfolding there different from that of Europe. It does not mean the death or absence of God, but a transformation of human self-understanding, giving men and women a new awareness of themselves as creative subjects or agents of history. The problem for the Church and theology is not how to deprivatize faith, but how to provoke a new social commitment of the Church, namely a use of its already influential position in society and culture on behalf of radical social change.

Second, political theology in Germany came on the scene as a critique of the current existentialist and personalist theologies, with their stress on individual decision and private, apolitical I–Thou relationships. The primary critical task of political theology was seen as the deprivatization of faith and theology. The starting-point of Latin American liberation theology was quite different. It began as a critique of developmentalism and of the latter's counterpart, Catholic liberalism. Developmentalism means 'the attempt to achieve social advances within existing structures and without altering these structures. Developmentalism originally referred only to economic achievement and industrial growth, but was broadened to include cultural and social progress as well' (Fiorenza, 1975: 17). As an approach to social change, developmentalism left intact existing political and economic structures with their injustices. The theology of liberation is an attempt to provide a Christian basis for a radical break with the *status quo* and a change to a new order of society.

Third, German political theology is primarily a new hermeneutic. In other words, it is chiefly concerned with the principles and methods for the interpretation of the Christian message in the context of modern society. The aim is to work out for theology the implications of the relationship between theory and practice. The questions it discusses are for the most part general, fundamental questions about Christian faith and social action. Metz himself has done little to give new political reinterpretations of the central ideas of Christian teaching (Bauer, 1976: 105 n. 155). Moreover, the interpretations he and Moltmann have given of particular Christian contents stand at one remove from practice. Political theology sees itself as the *theory* of a new *praxis*. What it says is linked to action, not directly, but only indirectly and mediately through political ethics. Latin American theology, in contrast, has been primarily concerned with giving interpretations of the Christian symbols of faith, so as to show their message of liberation.

15

Until Segundo's recent book, *The Liberation of Theology*, not much attention was paid to questions of method. Latin American theologians also wish to establish a more direct relation between Christian faith and political action than the Germans are prepared to admit.

The question of the relation between Christian faith and social action deserves separate treatment, and I return to it in chapter 3. I might simply note in passing that the objections against the abstract and theoretical character of German political theology parallel similar objections by the New Left against Habermas and indeed against the Frankfurt School of critical sociology in general (van den Oudenrijn, 1972: 64–6). Yet, it is precisely that School, particularly as represented by Habermas, which has been newly presenting and developing Marx's concept of the unity of theory and practice. Clearly, the matter will require some careful distinctions, such as those Habermas has suggested between critical theory and strategic political decisions.

Meanwhile, I want to consider an objection in the opposite direction, made against all forms of political theology and pressed particularly against Metz in Germany. It is that political theology represents an identification of the Christian message with particular political forms, so that it is no different in principle from the old-time confusion of religion and politics, except that it involves religion in the politics of the Left on behalf of social change rather than in the politics of the Right in support of the established order.

Admittedly, the name 'political theology', because of its history, immediately suggests the use of religion for political ends. The name goes back to Varro (116–27 BC) and his distinction of mythical theology, natural theology and political theology. Political theology meant the official and public religion of the State. With the conversion of the emperors, the official and public religion of the Roman Empire became Christian. Since that political takeover of the religion of the oppressed, Christian history has been dogged by a constant merging of religion and politics, a tendency which after the Middle Ages persisted through the Reformation and the period of the absolute monarchies and beyond that into various forms of Restoration thought. As for the name 'political theology', the use of it in the twentieth century prior to Metz is particularly unhappy. Carl Schmitt, lawyer and political theorist, who later became one of the intellectual counsellors of the Nazi regime, put forward a *politische Theologie* in a book under that title, published in 1922. His political theology meant the use of theological categories to legitimate political decisions and political regimes. He argued that the major political ideas of modern times were simply a transposition of essentially theological themes.

From the beginning of his enterprise of a new political theology, Metz (1973a: 107) has shown himself aware of the ambiguity of the name and of the misleading connotations with which it has been loaded historically. He has, however, stuck to it, despite suggestions for another name, such as 'public theology' or 'critical theology'. His conviction is that the provocative name forces people to confront the questions at issue. At the same time, he insists upon the difference between his new political theology and the older forms, and Moltmann has done the same in an essay giving a theological critique of political religion (1970; 11–51).

What, then, is the difference? If I may put it crudely in a way that calls for qualification: the old-time political theology was a sacralization of politics, the new political theology is a secularization of theology. Political theology of the old style was politics legitimated and served by religion. Religious symbols and religious authority were used to justify and support a particular political order. In the new political theology, it is politics that serve religion, in so far as it is in and through political and social action that religious faith is articulated and made effectual. The mediation of faith through politics does not imply any sacralization of politics. Politics are made sacred when an already articulated religious faith is applied to political ends, whereas if political activity is to be the medium in which religion comes to actuality and expression, it must have its own consistency as political. Again, the political mediation of faith does not give any particular political order or type of politics a unique or permanent status. Politics, when the cultural matrix of faith, will still remain transitory and changeable. The function given to politics in the new political theology tends, not to making politics sacred, but to making religion secular, in the sense of giving it expression in symbols and actions belonging to ordinary life rather than to a separate religious sphere.

The question is how far does the secularization go? Does it move toward a 'religionless Christianity', to borrow Bonhoeffer's phrase, merely in the sense of giving an expression to Christian faith that remains integrated into the everyday, instead of being set apart in a separate religious area of life? Or does it refuse to faith any dimension that is not identical with the temporal concerns of secular political action? If that is so, we do not have the idolatry of political religion in the sacralization of politics, but the worldliness of politics without religion, the complete dissolution of religion into politics. Religion will have proved itself to be ultimately illusory.

To put the question in a different way, How do we locate transcendence in social and political life? In what precise manner and in what precise place does the experience of transcendence emerge in society? When and how does political language become religious language and thus call for a theological interpretation? Max Horkheimer, a leading figure of the Frankfurt School, wrote: 'behind every genuine human action stands theology . . . a politics which, even when highly unreflected, does not preserve a theological moment in itself is, no matter how skilful, in the last analysis, mere business' (1975: 60). Political theology rightly reacts against seeing the locus of transcendence exclusively in the individual as a private person. Where, then, in the crowd of social concerns, actions and relationships does, in Horkheimer's phrase, 'die Sehnsucht nach dem ganz Anderen' (the longing for the Wholly Other) arise? Or, shall we say, When do people politically cease to be a crowd and become a common human subject in freedom?

Further discussion presupposes that we have clarified for ourselves the meaning of politics. Here, as Fierro (1977: 185) points out, Metz is disappointingly vague. He argues that a new political theology, avoiding the defects of the old, is possible, because the nature of politics has changed. He connects that change with the distinction between State and society, which he sees as a new feature of the modern period. Apart from that, his account of politics remains unclear. Xhaufflaire does discern some development in his thought. In Metz's first writings the term 'political' was synonymous with 'public' or 'social' in opposition to 'private' or 'individual'. The objections he met with on that score led him to merge the category of political with that of freedom, so that theological consciousness becomes political for Metz to the extent that it brings the Church and theology into relationship with the modern history of freedom (Xhaufflaire, 1972: 28). The modern history of freedom (*die neuzeitliche Freiheitsgeschichte*) is a key theme in Metz's thought. According to his conception of it, in the post-Enlightenment period the political order becomes an order of freedom and political consciousness a consciousness of freedom.

More helpful in reaching a concept of politics is an essay by Herbert Richardson, 'What makes a society political?' (*Religion and Political Society*, 1974: 95–120). He starts with a general notion of politics that does not restrict it to the process of gaining and exercising power within a society, but conceives it more generally as 'a practical enterprise devoted to creating a contingent and ever-changing order by compromising and balancing diverse and competing interests against one another' (*ibid.*, Introduction, 4). Making then a distinction between teleological values, which determine future goals and ultimate choices, and procedural or structural values, which determine the way society is organized in order to decide and pursue those goals and choices, he divides societies in terms of procedural values into two types: nonpolitical societies and political societies.

'In a nonpolitical society', he argues, 'government originates and presents itself as acting through a single will, or head. In a political society, government originates and presents itself as acting through a multitude of wills, or heads. Nonpolitical societies are monolithic; political societies are pluralistic' (*ibid.*, 101). Political society respects the integrity and freedom of the plurality of its constituent units, whether persons or groups. It aims at being a community; the will of its members cannot be expressed by a single will, but by a new kind of willing, a co-willing. The political activity it demands is not natural, but is a cultural creation, so that the emergence of political society requires the politicization of men and women. In political societies a new consciousness is necessary, a 'polyconsciousness' (*ibid.*, 113) with a capacity to bear plurality within itself and a power of empathy with others.

The religious faith of political community is faith in the transcendent. That is, the faith of political community is precisely that which excludes the absolutizing of any single will, group, or set of temporal goals. This means, too, that the faith of political community opposes all nonpolitical and immanentalistic forms of religion (*ibid.*, 114). So, not religion as such, which can be immanentist and absolutist, but faith in the transcendent is the foundation of political community and its values, and political society expresses its faith in the transcendent by its refusal to establish an official religion. The refusal protects the transcendence of its faith and its pluralism. A political society requires agreement on procedural, not on teleological values. It rests on a different conception of sovereignty to that of government by one will in nonpolitical society; its concept is that of 'a pluralized willing that is the communification of a plurality of wills' (*ibid.*, 105).

Richardson's account enables us to give a more precise content to Metz's association of politics with modern freedom. It also makes clear that the new political theology is not advocating a return to a monolithic order of society in which a single religion becomes the foundation for social action. The claim that faith in the transcendent is mediated through political action rests on the insight that politics, rightly conceived, is the realm of human freedom and community in the pursuit of values.

I have, however, a reservation to make about Richardson's account. He makes too sharp a distinction, it seems to me, between procedural and teleological values. Is it possible to secure agreement on procedural values, such as pluralism and freedom, without some measure of agreement on teleological values? He writes, 'Politics has nothing to do with visions of man's ideal end (eschatology)' (*ibid.*, 120). That statement is acceptable if he simply means that no single ultimate vision is imposed, but some accounts of human destiny, religious as well as nonreligious, would exclude his pluralistic view of politics as false and destructive. The faith in the transcendent on which he grounds his political society is itself grounded in a more determinate tradition concerning human goals and ultimate destiny, namely in a more determinate set of teleological values, than he is prepared to admit.

Procedural values, it should be stressed, are values, not just technical means. The existence of genuine politics is threatened today, not just by monolithic systems of government, but by the encroachment of a technocratic order that reduces social issues to questions of means. Politics, properly speaking, are about ends or values, and are therefore distinct from discussion about the rational adaptation of means to pre-given ends, which is the concern of technical debate among experts or technocrats.

That distinction between political and technical questions goes back to Aristotle's distinction between *praxis* and *poiesis*, between doing and making. 'Making' for Aristotle is an action with a tangible product, such as a ship or a table. '*Praxis*' refers to those actions, such as moral or social conduct, which have their meaning and end in themselves. 'Practical philosophy' is thus a philosophy of human affairs, dealing with moral and political action, that is with action considered normatively as concerned with the good and just life. Hence *praxis* and the practical in the narrow sense is distinct from *techne* or the skilful production of artefacts and the technical mastery such production presupposes.

However, a new habit of conceiving all human action on the model of a making or producing and the application of the techniques of empirical science to the knowledge and control of social processes have increasingly led to a conception of politics as the administration of society through the exercise of technical control. Politicians commend themselves as more likely to achieve the desired technical mastery in the solution of social problems than their opponents. So, the practical is confused with the technical, with the result that the practical in the Aristotelian sense of ends and values is virtually eliminated from public debate. There is no attempt to achieve a rational consensus, even in the pluralistic form of a compromise, in such matters. Instead, it is supposed that society can be run by technical reason alone, with destructive and inhuman results.

The problem I have broached of the elimination of the political by technocracy has been treated in some detail by

Habermas, and I will look in the next chapter at his analysis. I raise the matter here to make the point that political theology has to concern itself not just with the mediation of the transcendent through the political, but with the preservation of the political as an intrinsically human value. The two concerns are in fact linked.

Nevertheless, despite the worthiness of its aims and endeavours, the suspicion still nags that with political theology we are dealing with one more fad or passing fashion. Is it not, after all, still redolent of the sixties? All the key dates I quoted for its emergence were from that decade. That is where it would seem to belong. The sixties were the period of the civil rights movement, the counter-culture and the New Left, of student activism, protest and dissent, not merely in America, but in Europe. Dietrich Böhler looks back upon the fascination the writings of the Frankfurt School, of Horkheimer, Adorno, Marcuse and Benjamin, exercised over his student generation in Germany, sharing the influence of Ernst Bloch, who dominated the scene at the beginning of the sixties. When Horkheimer's *Eclipse of Reason*, first published in America in 1947, was republished in German in 1967, followed by his collection of essays, *Kritische Theorie*, in 1968, it was, Böhler says, as if a romantic, esoteric aura had been dispersed. These writings, now publicly available, had before been impossible to get hold of, always out of libraries, mimeographed and privately circulated. All who came out of school in search of social criticism and social ethics had come under the spell of the Frankfurt thinkers (Böhler, 1970a: 511). The spell now broke and questions took its place.

However, it is not merely that the student activists of the later sixties in Germany repudiated their earlier mentors in a return to a more traditional Marxism, but that the whole mood in the West has changed and moved away from those student activists themselves. Sometimes it seems as if the seventies have reversed every conviction, attitude and feeling of the sixties. In any event, the lack of interest in politics is such that one might borrow a term from writers on the spiritual life and speak of people as being in the grip of a political accidie. So, in theology, as a Dutch writer has observed, the recent theological trend is no longer 'political consciousness', but 'religious renaissance' (Schaeffer, 1972). Is, then, the interest embodied in political theology 'not only overdue but also too late' – to adapt the remark made by Christian Lenhardt (see O'Neill, ed. 1976: 34) about the recent flow of translations from the works of the Frankfurt School?

Before answering that question, I want to make a distinction between two levels of theological activity, which I will name original theology and scientific theology.

By original theology I mean theology as immediately bound up with religious living, a theology that accompanies action. Theology begins from Christian action. All human action is embodied meaning. Action as human is not a physical occurrence; it has a content of meaning. The same is true of Christian action; it has a content of Christian meaning. It is a way of life penetrated with religious meaning. In original theology that meaning is articulated in an articulation that remains embodied in action. The beliefs, norms and values presupposed by the Christian way of life are formulated explicitly and thus preached to the faithful and taught to children. Expositions of Christian faith are developed to help Christians live a Christian life. The stories and symbols and maxims are expounded, elaborated and applied; the inconsistencies in their meaning are ironed out; the doctrines are systematically set out in relation to one another and to other knowledge. All this theoretical work remains closely linked to action; it is the articulated consciousness of Christian practice.

I want to call that level of Christian thought original theology, because it is the creative source or origin for the rest of Christian thinking. We must come back again and again to the level of Christian action and to original theology as the consciousness intimately joined to that action. The other forms of Christian thinking are not in the same sense originative; they comment rather than create, and they depend on Christian action, and on original theology as the articulation of its consciousness, for their relationship with the realities of which Christian faith speaks.[6]

Original theology could also be called rhetorical theology, if one could remove the taint of artificiality and falseness from the word 'rhetoric', which properly means the art of persuasion. Original theology is rhetorical because it serves as a means of communication among men and women in action, as a form of mutual persuasion by which they are brought to engage in a common activity. That kind of theology constitutes and develops a particular tradition. What else is tradition but a set of common meanings, creating a common reference world and making possible common thoughts, common actions and common feelings? And such a community of meaning is maintained by a process of persuasive communication, namely rhetorically.

Thought, however, always tends to become methodical, or, in other words, scientific. 'Scientific' here has the wider sense of referring to any discipline or branch of knowledge that has developed an explicit method, not the narrow sense of referring to the empirical sciences. Theology, therefore, like other forms of knowledge has become methodical or scientific. Original theology has given rise to scientific theology.

The distinction I have sketched is made by Gutiérrez when he writes: 'Theology is reflection, a critical attitude. Theology *follows*; it is the second step. What Hegel used to say about philosophy can likewise be applied to theology: it rises only at sundown. The pastoral activity of the Church does not flow as a conclusion from theological premises. Theology does not produce pastoral activity; rather it reflects upon it' (1973: 11 – Gutiérrez's italics). It is used more forcibly by Fierro in saying: 'most of what has been written so far under the designation of "political theology" does not get beyond being merely theological language. It is the direct and spontaneous expression of a politically involved and committed faith, not second-stage critical reflection on that direct expression' (1977: 317). He insists: 'We can and must have a second-stage, reflexive, disciplined and critical language that focuses on first-stage theological language as its object and tries to work out its theoretical and scientific import. Only then do we have theology in the strict sense, which is not a language about God but a meta-language' (*ibid.*, 316).

In those quotations scientific or methodical theological reflection is simply designated as critical. I myself, however, would want to distinguish between scientific theology *tout court* and critical theology. Scientific theology simply as such is an elaboration and grounding of the Christian tradition as a place of truth and value and is thus historical and hermeneutical in its method. Critical theology acknowledges that the Christian tradition, like other traditions, is not exclusively a source of truth and value, but a vehicle of untruth and false values, and thus must be subjected to a critique of ideology and critically appropriated, not simply made one's own in an assimilative process of interpretation. But the need, possibility and method of a critical theology will recur as questions elsewhere in this book.[7]

Meanwhile, to return to the question, Is political theology already out of date? If taken on the first level of original theology, I think one must say that much of its writing is. Its rhetoric has dated. The mood of the sixties has gone. There is a sense that the political situation is more difficult and complex than previously supposed. There is an increased lack of self-confidence in tackling it. People have a sense that they personally need greater spiritual resources for social action. They have more respect for the richness of traditional religion. At the same time, they are vexed by the seemingly insoluble problem of effectively relating personal and political action, private and public life. Uncertainty, personal and political, marks the general tone. My remarks are impressionistic, but they might serve to indicate some of the reasons why the rhetoric of political theology irritates rather than helps many today.

That, however, does not allow us to dismiss political theology. First, because even at the rhetorical level, political theology in its various forms has become more subtle and nuanced and should not be identified with its earlier expressions. Second, more importantly, the problems raised and confronted by political theology as critical discourse are fundamental and ineluctable.

Put it in this way: theology has now lost its political innocence, just as it earlier lost its historical innocence with the rise of modern historiography. It took a long time for theology to awake to the disconcerting fact that looked at politically it had no clothes. The awakening to a critical political consciousness, to political maturity and guilt, was not helped by the undialectical negation of religion and theology by Feuerbach and Marx. At the level of critique political theology means the explicit

25

acknowledgement that the dialectic of theory and practice governs religious faith, and the working-out of the implications of that acknowledgement. The Marxist undialectical rejection of faith has been as much a block to that acknowledgement as the ideological stance of conservative churchmen. But once granted the dialectic of theory and practice as governing the realm of faith, the issues at stake are so basic that they cannot be subordinated to any changes of cultural mood or rhetorical emphasis.

Political theology, I have suggested, represents and articulates the end of doctrinal orthodoxy, just as in a parallel fashion historical theology and biblical criticism represented and articulated the end of literalism in interpretation. But if faith with its beliefs and norms is indeed mediated in practice and if practice is not the application of already known truths and norms, but that very process in and through which one comes to knowledge and values, then no particular faith can make an *a priori* claim to permanence and universality. Truth and values for human beings do not exist prior to practice. For that reason we have them yet only in part and as mired by social oppression. We still have to work for their greater emergence through social change. Permanence and universality in the realm of truth and value are desired achievements; they cannot be prior claims. Continuity in truth, which is the meaning of orthodoxy, is a hoped-for attainment; it cannot serve as a prior norm.

The practice that mediates faith is a social practice. Theology has also lost its political innocence in the recognition that there is no retreat to a private realm of religious experience. Any decision to withdraw from politics is itself a political decision, with political implications and consequences.

Nevertheless, if it was an insight of Marx that theory is not innocent, it is an insight of religion that practice is not innocent either. In discussing Habermas's attempt – which I will examine in chapter 4 – to ground freedom, justice and truth in an analysis of the ideal speech situation as presupposed and anticipated in all intersubjective communication, Bernstein remarks: 'What seems to be lacking here is any illumination on the problem of human agency and motivation. In a new form we have the old problem that has faced every critical theorist:

under what conditions will agents who have a clear under-standing of their historical situation be motivated to overcome distorted communication and strive toward an ideal form of community life?' (1976: 224). The primacy of practice, in par-ticular of emancipatory action, while destroying the theoretic confidence of orthodoxy, leads back to human interiority and motivation, to questions of moral impotence and salvation: in theological terms, to sin and grace.

But that, perhaps, is too easy a transposition. Critical theo-logy must follow the exigencies of rational discourse, not the immediate needs of a particular way of life. Hence, it has to look to the title-deeds before redecorating the house.

2

The acceptance of modernity

Modernity has commonly been a problem for authoritative religion. It has certainly been so for Church Christianity, which denounced all heretics as *innovatores*. To take a few key examples of the modern:

The *via moderna* of Ockham, whom Heer calls 'the founder of modern European democracy' (1966: 168), was a threat to the Curial order, whereas the *via antiqua* of Thomists and Scotists was its support. Heer draws a contrast between medieval realism and Ockham's nominalism. Realism, in the fashion common to traditional societies, saw 'thinking as an expression of being' and words as given in the sacral–political order of the universe. For Ockham, 'language was now to be a democratic convention between free individuals, who reach understanding between themselves on the meaning of each word and concept' (*ibid.*, 167). This strongly reminds one of the contrast between Heidegger and Gadamer on the one hand and Enlightenment reason and positivism on the other. But what is more relevant here is to notice that Ockham's 'group egoism' or emphasis upon the freedom of groups was 'a sober, factual presentation of the political and social realities' of his time (*ibid.*, 169). His thought, that is, was modern in the sense of grounded in the present.

The communities of brethren, initiated by Gerhard Groote in the fourteenth century, with their *devotio moderna*, aroused much opposition from the traditional religious Orders, despite their own peacefulness. Their outlook was felt as a silent criticism. Why? 'At the root of everything', writes Southern, 'there was a persistent desire for experiment, a desire to discover for oneself a way of life suited to one's own experience' (1970: 344). In short, there was an independence from the past with its traditions and a desire for the present with its immediately experienced.

Then at the Enlightenment emerged that sense of modernity which still pervades our mentality and culture. Peter Gay in comparing the Enlightenment philosophes to the Renaissance humanists remarks that the 'philosophes reveled in their age because they were witnessing the triumphs of the scientific intellect' (1966: 269). Thus at the beginning of the modern age lies the scientific revolution of the last one-third of the seventeenth century. The emergence of modern science may not indeed be the fundamental novelty, but may itself be the effect of some deeper change. Yet, whatever the interpretation of the total event, the scientific revolution, taken with its social and political causes and consequences, may be used to mark an upheaval so great that it created a sense that the modern world was different in kind, not only from its own past, but from that of all other cultures.

And what makes the modern age modern *par excellence* is its making decisive the actuality of the observable and experimental, in place of a traditional and authoritative past. Its world is empirical, subject to natural laws, but open to change and improvement – a product of human making, like smaller artefacts. The modern world is not a normative, pre-given order to which one must conform. Hence the persistent sense of newness and difference from all other cultures as traditional. Wilfred Cantwell Smith points out that 'the emergence of Hinduism and Islam as "traditional religions" is itself a symptom of modern culture' (1976: 66). Other cultures have thus been marked as traditional by the thrust of modernity.

What, then, is modernity? It is to ground culture upon the present. That is why it is anathema to dogmatic Christianity. Concern with the present reality of men is always undogmatic, as Trutz Rendtorff remarks (1969: 80–2). Unlike modernity, dogmatism grounds itself upon the past as normative. Modernity may look to the past as the philosophes looked over the Middle Ages to pagan antiquity, but dogmatism claims to interpret the present in the light of the past (how far it can and does achieve this is another question), whereas modernity interprets the past in the light of the present. All modernity further becomes anti-dogmatic, because it is an appeal to the present against the past.

But the matter is not so straightforward as that. The modern age has its specific modernity from its identification of present reality with the observable, the empirical. There has been an exclusion of a nonempirical present. The exclusion is partly explicable by the continued identification of the metaphysical and religious with a dogmatic assertion of past tradition as authoritative. But whatever the underlying reasons, it has resulted in a further narrowing. The empirical itself has been largely treated as merely the technically controllable and human action has been reduced to manipulable behaviour, even to the denial of consciousness. The distinction between *poiesis* and *praxis* has been lost. *Poiesis* is making, and to it belongs *techne*, the rational adaptation of means to pre-given ends. *Praxis* is distinctively human doing, constituted by the deliberation and choice of ends. If all human action is conceived as *poiesis*, controllable by *techne*, so that *praxis* is ignored or eliminated, there is no freedom and no political discussion of ends. The experts become technocrats, ruling with an authority that cannot be challenged, except by other experts on technical grounds. Modernity is thus leading to the unfreedom of a society unable to question the expertise of bureaucrats and technocrats. The empirical present is proving as narrow a prison as the dogmatic past.

There are those who consider – and the point is as old as the Romantic reaction against the Enlightenment – that only the sense of belonging to a tradition can overcome the arrogant inhumanity of technical reason. A human community lives from its tradition, the memory of things past embodied in its language, its myths, its institutions. Without tradition there is no human consciousness. Are we, then, to turn back from modernity to a renewed acceptance of the past as normative, that is to dogmatism?

The suggestion of Metz and Moltmann, both inspired by Ernst Bloch, is that neither the past nor the present are rightly conceived without reference to the future. It is when we grasp past and present as openness to the future that we understand them as history not nature, as the realm of human freedom not of natural necessity. In an essay, 'The responsibility of hope', Metz turns away from metaphysics because of its neglect of history:

The obfuscation of the future in metaphysics includes the obfuscation of all history, for the future is what constitutes history as history.
As long as history is thought of primarily as past and present, it can
be thought of as a reality that has taken place or is taking place now,
and thus can be understood as nature and ontologized. Only with
reference to the future can historical reality be distinguished from
nature (1960: 282).

Freedom is the soul of all history, and to be free is to be open
to the future. Technological development is openness to the
future as genuinely new only in so far as it serves human subjects and their freedom. When it dominates as master it
becomes the stabilizing and reinforcement of the present. The
dystopias of science fiction are completely programmed
orders where openness to the future has been closed off. Technology as such deals with natural necessity, not with freedom.

Both the dogmatic fixation of the past and the technical pro-
gramming of the present are thus a denial of the human subject. But was it not the discovery of the human subject with its
freedom that constituted the transition to modernity? Is not
the freedom of human subjects to make themselves and their
world, instead of conforming to a pre-given order as sacred, a
more essential characteristic of modernity than empirical
rationality?

I have broached the problem of modernity because political
theology presents itself as both an acceptance and a theory of
the present modern age.

It is an acceptance. Although political theology is within the
critical tradition and relates itself to modern society as a critique, it is in a prior way an acceptance of modernity, because
part of what distinguishes it as a new theological beginning is
its reversal of the long-standing blank rejection of the modern
world by the Churches. Its critique of society belongs itself to
its modernity.

The negative relation between the Churches and the
modern world has been given expression in the concept of
secularization. 'Secularization' is an elusive term. It was introduced by the French in the negotiations for the Peace of West-
phalia (1648), which brought the Thirty Years War to an end.

There it meant the alienation of Church property. Max Weber and Ernst Troeltsch took it over and made it into a descriptive and analytical term for the study of modern society. Since then it has made swift though drunken progress down the highways of sociology and theology. Some sociologists, like David Martin (1969: 22), and theologians, like Trutz Rendtorff (1969: 22), feel that the time has come to disqualify it.

Others have tried to bring it to order. Larry Shiner (1967: 207–20) distinguishes six meanings of secularization, namely: the decline of religion, the shift of attention to this world, the disengagement of society from religion, the transposition of religious beliefs and institutions into products of human making and responsibility, the desacralization of the world, the movement from a fixed sacral order to the acceptance of social change. The difficulty comes when one tries to apply these meanings. The application in each case requires a criterion or norm and a factual assessment, and each time both of these are open to considerable dispute. Take the first instance: the decline of religion. To assert that religion declined with the rise of the modern world presupposes a particular concept of religion as normative and that a factual investigation shows that religion in that sense has indeed declined. Agreement on neither point is easy to reach. Again, the second meaning – the shift of attention to this world – presupposes that one has delimited the concept of this world and established that attention to it was less in the past than at present. Agreement here might prove easier, but I doubt whether it can be counted upon.

We move in a clearer direction if we limit our attention to the Christian Churches and the change in their relation to society between the Middle Ages and modern times, without evaluating that change as a decline or progress in the Christian religion, let alone in religion in a wider sense.

That there has been a change in the relationship between Church and society is indisputable. The medievalist Southern wrote: 'The identification of the church with the whole of organized society is the fundamental feature which distinguishes the Middle Ages from earlier and later periods of history' (1970: 16). The medieval *corpus christianum* absorbed all political and socio-cultural elements into itself. No distinction was made between the Church and society. The Church was the total society. In other words, medieval society corresponds to what the political scientist Donald Eugene Smith (1970) analyses as a traditional religio-political system. In such a system the political community is identical with the religious community in theory and substantially so in fact, the religious ideas of the community legitimate the power structure and the religiously integrated and legitimated social system, not an efficient governmental apparatus, is the chief means of social control. Such was the medieval religio-political system, usually named Christendom. Then, in various stages, this broke up. The Churches became separated from the polity, which sought its legitimation elsewhere. Major areas of social life, such as education, law, economy and so on passed from regulation by the Churches to the jurisdiction of the State. By the end of the loss of power, the Churches had changed from public institutions into voluntary associations, functioning within the private sphere. Needless to say, the process was not entirely rectilinear, but subject to twists and inconsistencies.

The first breach in the unity of Christendom came about as a result of the Investiture Struggles of the eleventh century. These originated, it will be remembered, from the refusal of the pope to allow the temporal ruler, notably the emperor, to invest bishops with their insignia of office, an investiture being a sign of feudal subordination. The victory of Pope Gregory VII in excluding the emperor from ecclesiastical investitures caused a first separation of State from Church. In the controversy the Church as a hierarchical, sacramental institution was distinguished from the Christian world as a whole, the *orbis christianus*, which had been the older meaning of Church or *ecclesia*. The emperor as emperor was now outside the more narrowly defined *ecclesia*, and so the Empire became a secular reality. Secular here is understood in contrast to sacred when this is identified with what belongs to the Church. The Empire was not indeed fully secular, because the Church continued to claim and exercise a higher dominion. This was justified on grounds of man's sinfulness, *ratione peccati*. Man's sin had left his natural powers in need of healing grace for their proper functioning and thus subordinated them to the hierarchical Church as the source of grace. In other words, the papal monarchy still claimed supremacy over the whole Christian world. Nevertheless, the paradoxical effect of the papal victory in the matter of investitures was the liberation – still partial – of the political sphere as secular.

The distinction between State and Church carried a cultural counterpart with it. The division between lay and clerical culture began at that time. It lies at the origin of the polarization of culture into secular and religious, which has been a peculiar feature of the Western world.

By breaking the unity of the Christian Church in the West and by denying the papal supremacy the Reformation was undoubtedly a stage in the disintegration of Christendom. However, the medieval ideal of a unified Christian society was not radically questioned. The radical change came as a result of the Religious Wars, unleashed by the Reformation. These wars brought a reversal of the power relations between Church and State and led the State to seek its legitimation outside Christian truth as entrusted to the Church. The ecclesiastical authorities proved themselves incapable of assuring peace. Consequently, the political realm now emancipated itself from the religious. It was the State that now claimed dominion over the Churches: *Cuius regio, illius religio*. At the same time, for the political and social order men sought a basis independent of the Christian revelation, seen as the cause of unending bloody conflicts. Hence the rise of the modern natural law theories, beginning with Hugh de Groot's *De jure belli et pacis* of 1625 (Hazard, 1973: 306–25).

This development brought the secularization of the State, namely the legitimation of its power structure without appeal to the Christian religion as embodied in the Churches. Secular political theories from the seventeenth century onward offered the State a legitimation of its power structure other than that previously given by integration into the totality of Christendom. Christendom now ceased to be a credible articulation of the actual reality of Western society and instead took on the role of an ideal cherished by Christians.

The State in this fashion emerged as the totality within which the Churches were elements. It expanded its power at the expense of the Churches over various areas of social life.

But the Churches, especially the Catholic Church, refused absorption into the State as totality. Their acceptance *de facto* of a measure of control by the political power was regarded as a compromise. The return to Christendom, namely to a social and political order in which Christian authority would once more have dominion, remained the ideal. The result in practice was that the Churches struggled to keep or regain control in any social or political area where this remained feasible.

That situation of uneasy compromise between Church and State has had a twofold cultural consequence. The general culture of the West has been shot through with strongly negative attitudes to religion, ranging from anti-clericalism through anti-Christianity to anti-religion. On the other hand, specifically Christian culture within the Churches has been marked by a negative attitude to the modern world. As Metz himself admits, 'there is hardly one idea of critical societal importance in our history – take Revolution, Enlightenment, Reason, or again – Love, Liberty – which was not at least once disavowed by historical Christianity and its institutions' (1973a: 117). The rejection of modern liberties by the Syllabus of Pius IX is well known. But this was not an isolated incident. When the historian E. E. Y. Hales was studying the background to what he called 'the Revolution of Pope John', he found that John XXIII was indeed the very first pope to speak positively of the modern world (1965: 27–37).

There has, then, undeniably been a conflict between the Churches and the modern political and social order, with a loss of power and position on the side of the Churches. This has led to a rejection of the modern world by the Churches and a rejection of Christianity as represented by the Churches on the part of many modern people. Both sides interpret the rise of modernity as secularization, understood evaluatively as a movement away from the Christian religion. But is not this a false evaluation? Cannot the modern world be seen as the deepening and maturing of Christian ideals and values, together with the casting-off of their now inadequate medieval embodiment in the Churches as authority structures?

Political theology, as I have said, puts itself forward as an acceptance of modernity. In doing so, it offers a theory of the present modern age to replace the dominant interpretation of it by both secularists and Christians as a decline of the Christian religion. There was, however, a forerunner to political theology as a positive Christian interpretation of modernity, namely the theology of secularization. I must say something about that earlier theology before examining the more complex account political theology gives of the modern world.

The themes of the theology of secularization or secular theology have been around for some time. They were made popular in the English-speaking world by Harvey Cox in *The Secular City*. But the writer who gave them their systematic expression was the Protestant theologian Friedrich Gogarten, chiefly in his book *Despair and Hope For Our Time*. It is with Gogarten's thought I am here concerned.

In the most general terms, the theology of secularization not merely rejects the assumption that there is an incompatibility between the Christian faith and the modern secularized world, but argues that modern secularity is the legitimate and necessary outcome of the Christian faith itself. 'Secularization' paradoxically now becomes a word with a positive religious meaning.

Here, however, Gogarten distinguishes two meanings of secularization: the secularization of faith and the secularization of the world. The first, the secularization of faith, otherwise called secularism, is a false secularization, of which man is the agent and faith the object. It is an attempt by sinful man to claim what belongs only to faith and thus to put man in God's place. It either produces ideologies of worldly salvation or falls into nihilism. The secularization of the world, on the other hand, has God as agent and the world itself, not faith, as object. Gogarten expresses the process he has in mind by the reduplicative expressions, 'the world becoming world' (*Verweltlichung der Welt*) and 'the historization of history' (*Vergeschichtlichung der Geschichte*). The Christian acknowledgement of the non-worldly character of faith cleanses the world from false religion and thus frees the world for its worldliness and allows history to be genuinely history. In that sense the modern secular world as secular is the legitimate effect of the Christian faith. Gogarten thus pulls apart Christian faith and the world, divine history or revelation on the one hand and world-history on the other. Faith is not mediated through the world and its history; it is, as Gogarten puts it, 'a matter of decision made immediately and exclusively in the context of the personal relation to God' (1970: 121). For Gogarten the duality he sets up is a simple application of the distinction between faith and works, grace and law. Larry Shiner thus sums up the matter in his Foreword to *Despair and Hope for Our Time*:

Faith is directed exclusively to the hidden being of God; works are directed exclusively to the world and in no way affect faith nor are they affected by it since they are given over to the independent decision of reason. Faith cannot influence 'what' particular works are done but only 'how' they are done. It keeps works from being carried out with the intention of realizing the wholeness of man's being or giving a final meaning to his existence. In this way man's entire active life in the world becomes a matter of human responsibility, it becomes 'secular'. By sharply and incessantly distinguishing man's history with God occurring in faith from his history with the world as it occurs through reason, Gogarten makes secularization the counterpart of faith (1970: 3).

In other words, the world, its history and its concerns, is a matter of works and law. Works and law are legitimate in their place, but we are justified by faith, not by works, by grace, not by law. The secularization of the world is simply the consequence of the principle of justification by faith alone; it is the elimination of the efforts of sinful man to justify himself by religious works.

There is a link, however, between the two orders of faith and works, faith and the world. The point of union is found in Christian man himself as God's son. By faith man has entered into his inheritance as son; he is no longer slave or infant. As son he has been given two freedoms, a freedom for God in faith and a freedom of works to care for the world. The second freedom is what has come to fruition in the autonomy claimed by secular man over against the attempts to enclose him in fixed mythical, metaphysical and religious world-views. God has put him as an independent adult in possession of this world.

Christian faith, therefore, cannot serve as a source of ethical principles by which to determine what works are to be done. Nor does Christian faith give man any answer he can articulate to the questions concerning the meaning of human existence and world-history. He is left in the condition of 'ignorant questioning'. In a sense faith hears the answer, but that answer remains inscrutable and beyond understanding. As God's gift, it is not at man's disposal. 'If this answer', writes Gogarten, 'were not unsearchable for faith and not preserved as God's futurity, it would no longer be the answer of the God who brings life from death, and faith would no longer be faith' (1970: 150–1). Faith, therefore, must not be transformed into a system of beliefs or a set of ethical demands.

In developing that point, Gogarten makes a distinction between Christian faith and Christianity. Unlike Christian faith, Christianity is a purely historical phenomenon. To identify it with faith would be to secularize that faith and fall into a 'Christian secularism'. Christianity, he asserts, 'represents the various manifestations of the human spirit which have emerged as a result of man's liberation, through the faith, from the mythical enclosure by the world' (*ibid.*, 142). These manifestations have been rightly secularized in the course of history, because when unsecularized and confused with faith, they embody two misunderstandings of Christian faith, namely the moralistic one of treating faith as a pattern for man's action and the metaphysical one of making faith into an allegedly revealed world-view. Since the Churches have promoted both these misunderstandings, it is not surprising that more of Christian freedom is found outside them than within (Shiner, 1966: 35–41).

Many people have picked up a mistaken idea of the theology of secularization, supposing its general bearing to be a close linking of faith and secular concerns. In fact, for the theology of secularization every attempt to mediate faith and civilization, faith and knowledge, faith and substantive ethical norms, represents an impossible and illegitimate attempt to secularize faith – a perversion of faith that by Gogarten's own account began in the New Testament itself with the incorporation of mythical and gnostic elements.

To conclude this brief account of the theology of secularization, I want to disengage two basic conceptions it would seem to imply: the first is its purely spiritual and personal understanding of Christian faith. This faith is made into a purely private event or decision. The concept of faith as a personal, spiritual act is in effect so formal that faith cannot be given any content at all without inconsistency. An objective content, however slight, would insert faith into world-history and take away the duality upon which the theology of secularization rests.

The second conception is an implied view of world-history that regards it as an irreversible process of rationalization, moving from an age of myth and metaphysics to the modern secular age of science and technology. Despite Gogarten's talk of freedom, this is a positivistic and deterministic conception of history, reminiscent of Comte.

The theology of secularization is not just an elaboration of themes internal to theology, but a theory of the present modern age. If so, how far is it empirically verifiable or falsifiable? Gogarten declares that his analysis surpasses the historical viewpoint and concerns the essence of the Christian faith. The danger, however, of such an *a priori* interpretation of the modern world is shown if we consider the contention of Frans van den Oudenrijn (Xhaufflaire and Derksen, 1970: 155–72) that the theology of secularization represents an uncritical acceptance of late capitalist society. In other words, it is the religious ideology of technocratic society.

The point he makes is seen by contrasting Gogarten's account of modernity with the analyses of capitalist society given by Macpherson (1975) and Habermas (1971c and 1976a). It is worth expounding these at some length.

Macpherson analyses the ideology of liberal, bourgeois society in its historical origins as 'possessive individualism'. The new belief in the value and rights of the individual was possessive in form, the individual being conceived as essentially the proprietor of his own person or capacities, owing nothing to society for them. Freedom was a function of possession, so that the individual was free as owner of himself. Society became a number of free, equal individuals related to each other as proprietors of their own capacities and of whatever they have acquired by the exercise of those capacities. In other words, society consisted of relations of exchange among independent proprietors. It was a market view of society, because society was constituted by a set of market relationships. What makes the individual free is his freedom from any dependence upon others outside that of self-interested contractual relationship.

Such a society, Habermas points out, was legitimated, that is, its authority justified as valid, by the ideology of just exchange, namely by the claim that there was an exchange equivalence between capital and wage-labour, secured by the operation of a free market. Wage-labourers were able to sell their labour on the open market, and were therefore considered as sharing in the proprietorial freedom enjoyed by all individual members of the society. Other components, besides just exchange, entered into the total complex of bourgeois ideology. There was the ideology of achievement, according to which rewards were and should be distributed on the basis of individual achievement. This was expressed in the Horatio Alger myth[8] and in competitive occupational and educational systems. There was also the use made of the utilitarian principles of Jeremy Bentham, who, in making the fundamental principle of morality the greatest happiness of the greatest number, maintained that self-interests, properly understood, do not clash and that personal happiness and general welfare go together.

Bourgeois ideology was not, need it be said, Christian, but a cause of great confusion was that it was never self-sufficient. Christianity thus provided its context and some additional support. The appeal to traditional religion continued when it was a question of facing the basic negativities of life, namely guilt, sickness and death. Again, traditional elements were used to provide supplementary motivation. The Protestant ethic, with its emphasis upon self-discipline, its vocational ethos and its policy of renouncing immediate gratification, helped to form the achievement ethos of the middle classes, while other elements from the religious tradition strengthened the obedience and fatalism of the lower classes and encouraged their tendency to immediate gratification.

Habermas sees a crisis of legitimation now occurring in advanced capitalist society, because the ideology of just exchange through the operation of the free market has become untenable on account of the reintroduction of State intervention in the economic order. The political order can no longer be legitimated by the economic order as before when political power was justified as the means of securing the free market. Now that the State massively intervenes in economic affairs, it again needs legitimation in its own right. This, according to Habermas, cannot be provided by the traditional world-views, which have in the course of capitalist development gradually lost their efficacy, owing to the rationalization of areas of life formerly regulated by tradition and to the incompatibility of the traditional world-views with the cognitive attitudes derived from science. Hence the present trend is to provide the required legitimation by making science and technology an ideology. In other words, society has become technocratic, in as much as all questions of policy are presented as technical questions to be dealt with in terms of a means–end rationality. The distinction between the technical and the practical, between purposive rational action and communicative action based on values is eliminated. The technocratic form of social order demands a depoliticization of the mass of the population, because the solution of technical problems cannot be a matter of public discussion. For society thus to be legitimated by technical reason, the depoliticization has to be accepted by a diffusion of technocratic consciousness among people in general.

The transition from a bourgeois, liberal society to a late capitalist, technocratic society is mirrored in the rise and subsequent breakdown of the bourgeois public sphere (Habermas, 1962). The bourgeois public sphere was a new historical reality when it emerged in England at the end of the seventeenth century and in France in the eighteenth century. The distinction between a public and a private sphere did not obtain in medieval feudal society. There was a representative publicness, such as that of king or bishop, but this publicness consisted in a public representation of dominion or rule; it did not constitute a social sphere over against another social sphere, the private. The development of the modern State with its permanent administrative organization brought a distinction between the sphere of the public power of the State and the private sphere, to which belonged all those people not holding State office or other official position. But this latter sphere, the sphere of industry and commerce, of general opinion and discussion, was of social relevance; it constituted civil society as

41

now distinct from the State. In civil society there emerged the bourgeois public. It was the 'public' addressed by the State, but yet a public of private people, corresponding therefore as a social development to the individualism of bourgeois ideology. The bourgeois public saw the formation of public opinion and the opening-up of various areas of social life, such as religion or the family, to critical discussion. Whereas formal discourse or rhetoric had been the language and medium of representative publicness, the political language and medium of the bourgeois public was open, public reasoning. Together with public argument as a political medium came the institutions of freedom of assembly, freedom of association and freedom of speech.

The bourgeois public was a development unique in history. Nevertheless, although it did mark an advance in human social and political life, it did not mean the achievement of a social communication undistorted by domination. The openness of discourse, like the freedom of the market, concealed the actual inequality of persons and the economically based structure of power. Civil society as a public sphere was in fact the arena for the pursuit of individual and class interests. Civil rights gave freedom to the capitalist entrepreneurs, but the individual in bourgeois society, with its possessive individualism, was not truly free as a citizen to enter into a genuine community with fellow citizens.

Whatever its good or bad qualities, the bourgeois public has now disintegrated with the evolution of the bourgeois economy. The entrepreneurs have been swallowed by the large corporations, within which discussion is not public, but is limited to technicians and bureaucrats. Public opinion outside is manipulated, and the public is no longer an arena for critical discussion among persons. At present with the trend to technocracy, society manifests what Habermas calls a syndrome of civil, familial and vocational privatism. Civil privatism means that people are expected to have an interest in the government and administration of society, but without being given a real share in the decision-making process. Genuine participation or substantive democracy has been replaced by formal democracy, namely formally democratic institutions and procedures, but used to elicit a diffuse mass loyalty, while avoiding public involvement in specific administrative decisions. The public realm has been depoliticized. Hence civil privatism. Familial and vocational privatism combine an orientation to the family, focussing upon consumption and leisure, with a career orientation. Bourgeois culture has become a culture of consumers.

With Habermas's account of the evolution of modern society in mind, let us now turn back to Gogarten's theology of secularization. Its basic conception of faith as a purely private event or decision merely articulates what happened to the Christian religion in modern society. When the distinction arose between the State as public and civil society as essentially private, religion fell into the private sphere. Since then, it has become increasingly a private, subjective matter. Instead of questioning the dualism of public and private spheres, which has deprived people of their role as citizens to make society a genuine community, with common ends and spiritual values, the theology of secularization capitulates and allows faith to be thrust out of society and world-history into a purely individual and family realm. It serves as an ideological reinforcement of the present depoliticization of the people and public opinion. Again, technocratic society as described by Habermas corresponds pretty closely to the secular world of the theologians of secularization. The disenchanted secular world, extolled by them as liberated from false religion into its autonomy, is the one-dimensional world as seen exclusively in terms of scientific and technical reason by modern technocrats.

All, then, that Gogarten would seem to have done is to have translated the attitudes and values of contemporary society into theological jargon. Not that I regard the analyses of Habermas and others like him as beyond dispute. But at least their interpretation is open to verification or falsification with reference to the data they present. Gogarten gives us theological concepts and wide unsupported generalizations. Does political theology do any better?

Metz's theory of modernity has passed through several stages. He himself has given an assessment of his own theological development in regard to modernity, suggesting that it might serve as a type for theology in general. First came the book *Christliche Anthropozentrik*, published in 1962, representing a general acceptance of modernity. Then in the second place appeared the essays collected in the first half of *Theology of the World*, which put forward an abstract thesis on secularization. Finally, political theology has related the Christian faith to social *praxis* and the modern history of freedom (Metz, Moltmann, Oelmüller, 1970: 66 n. 28).

Metz's *Christliche Anthropozentrik*, subtitled *Über die Denkform des Thomas von Aquin*, is not just a fresh interpretation of St Thomas. It is, more strikingly, a thesis about the fundamentally Christian character of the modern age and modern philosophy. The book is built upon a distinction between the content of thought and its formal structure, namely its *Denkform* or thought-form. A thought-form is the understanding of being which penetrates all that is thought and which also establishes the horizon within which the thinking occurs. Metz proceeds to set up an opposition between the cosmocentric thought-form of the Greeks and the anthropocentric thought-form of Thomas Aquinas.

Although the anthropocentric thought-form in Thomas remains overlaid and concealed by categories drawn from the culturally still-dominant cosmocentric thought-form, some decisive indications show that Thomas's thinking represents a fundamental shift. This shift is nothing less than the beginning of modernity. It opened an epoch and ushered in modern thought. Thomas Aquinas is for that reason the turning-point between Greek and modern thinking (1962: 122). He is the 'father of modern thought' (*ibid.*, 123), because at the basis of modern philosophy is the anthropocentric thought-form introduced by Thomas.

The anthropocentric thought-form for Metz thus serves the same function as the Pauline distinction between law and grace, faith and works, for Gogarten: namely as the Christian point of origin for modern thought and culture. Both theses can be equally criticized as substituting conceptual analysis for concrete history and attempting to explain the modern world simply in terms of thought. Moreover, it is questionable whether the anthropocentric shift represents the fundamental movement of modernity or merely a half-way house in the transition from supernatural, religious myth and pure theory on the one hand to empirical rationality and practically mediated theory on the other.

In the second transitional stage of his thought, Metz put forward a theology of secularization, based upon an unusual interpretation of the Incarnation. Metz denies any dependence upon Gogarten, although he shows a familiarity with his work (Bauer, 1976: 14 n. 27).

The Incarnation for Metz is God's definitive acceptance of the world and man. It is not, as it is so often interpreted to be, the divinization of the world, but the liberation of the world in its specific character as world. Through the Incarnation the world appears for the first time as completely worldly and God as completely divine. What God makes his own in the Incarnation is the world in its non-divinity as radically different from him (1973a: 29).

Secularization in the perspective of the Incarnation is the transition from a divinized to a hominized world, which meant the emergence of the free subjectivity of men in history. That was possible only because the world was experienced under the eschatological horizon of hope. Under a transcendent hope, the world becomes subject to change by the free activity of men. It is no longer a fixed, sacrosanct reality, but an emergent reality open to the future and the genuinely new. Here Metz's thought links up with that of Moltmann, and both share a common dependence upon Ernst Bloch.[9] For Metz, therefore, secularization is the process of change and innovation in the world through the activity of human freedom (1973a: 91).

At this stage of his theology, however, Metz, like Gogarten, removed faith as transcendent from concrete history. That is made clear in his article, 'Unbelief as a theological problem' (1965b). Faith is there presented as 'a free and imponderable gift of grace according to divine predestination', which is never man's 'disponible possession' (*ibid.*, 63). There is an 'infinite difference between the mental images and concepts formed from experience in this world on the one hand, and the truths of faith described in terms of those concepts' (*ibid.*, 66). The secularization of the world 'has given us a heightened sense of the impossibility of visualizing the things of faith and their super-categoriality. All world-derived concepts and propositional objectivations of our faith are also essentially concealing in character' (*ibid.*, 67). The experience of faith is concealed; belief and unbelief so penetrate each other in human consciousness that they cannot be separated in the concrete. Thus Metz puts faith over against the world and history and refuses a mediation of faith through concrete social reality. His theology at this stage is open to the same criticisms as Gogarten's.

Nevertheless, Metz had always shown concern with history, with history as specifically distinct from nature, with history as directed to the future by eschatological hope. It was that concern with history which eventually led to Metz's break with the transcendental anthropology of Rahner (Mann, 1969–70) and to his own proclamation of a 'political theology'.

At the basis of Metz's concept of political theology as a new, required phase of Christian theology is the thesis that in the age of Enlightenment the political order emerged clearly and effectively as an order of freedom. From that time onward, political structures and institutions were no longer seen as prior to man's freedom, but as founded upon human freedom and consequently as changing and changeable (Metz, 1969b: 270). With the *Aufklärung* political consciousness becomes a consciousness of liberty.

Metz's theory of modernity is now a thesis about what he calls the modern history of freedom (*die neuzeitliche Freiheitsgeschichte*). We may note with Moltmann (1969: xii) that the German term *Neuzeit*, probably first used by Heinrich Heine in the nineteenth century, means more than 'modern times' and implies messianic expectations in a way similar to the parallel expression 'new world'. In speaking of the modern history of freedom Metz does not mean that freedom was not a theme in the earlier epochs of the Western tradition. What he does contend, however, is that in the modern epoch freedom is no longer just one theme among others; freedom has now become the central and fundamental theme of our culture. Further, it is now given expression, not only abstractly as man's free subjectivity and his dominance as a subject over nature, but concretely in its religious, social, political and economic institutions and modes of life (Metz, Moltmann, Oelmüller, 1970: 61).

Modern freedom implies the secularization of politics, namely the recognition that the political order is not part of a pre-ordained and sacred order, but is created freely by men. That is why the new political theology does not carry any desire with it to bring the political order once again under the Church. On the contrary, presupposing the secularization of politics, the aim of the new political theology is to bring the Church and theology into a positive relation with the modern history of secular freedom. How, then, are secular politics and theology related?

In an order of freedom political consciousness is inevitably confronted with the problem of change in political institutions. Consequently, any critical political consciousness has to remain aware of the social foundations of the order of freedom with its changing institutions. These foundations reach back into the history of freedom. There in the origins and history of freedom is where political consciousness meets theology. On its part, theological consciousness, in virtue of its message of liberation, is concerned with the history of freedom. Since the history of freedom has now become political and freedom the immanent foundation of the political order, theological consciousness must itself become political, in order to retain its relationship with the ongoing history of freedom (Metz, 1969b: 270–1).

Is Metz's theory of modernity as the emergence of social and political freedom merely an uncritical acceptance of secularist claims and a belated canonization of the liberal conception of progress by a Catholic theologian? Metz rebuts all such objections as a misunderstanding of his position. He repeatedly insists upon a dialectical understanding of the modern history of freedom. Indeed for him the idea of a unilinear development of ever greater freedom is excluded by the very concept of freedom-history (*Freiheitsgeschichte*), because a teleological evolutionary progress contradicts the meaning of history as history (Metz, Moltmann, Oelmüller, 1970: 62 n. 21). Only nature is or can be realized according to an immanent end or *telos*. History as such is essentially unfulfillable; it cannot be conceived in terms of immanence. The immanence–transcendence scheme, which is derived from the classical metaphysics of nature, is inapplicable to historical reality and its future. There is not nor can be an inner-historical fulfilment of history or progress towards such an end. History as history is open and has no immanent end. In his most recent book, *Glaube in Geschichte und Gesellschaft*, Metz, under the banner of apocalyptic as a consciousness of the catastrophic, non-teleological nature of history, launches a full-scale attack upon what he considers the ideological symbol of evolution (1977a: 149–58).

Moreover, Metz is aware that, as he says, 'we cannot and must not simply *identify* the actual modern process of secularization with the secularity of the world that Christ made possible and intended' (1973a: 41 – Metz's italics). He insists, then, upon the ambiguity of modernity and the need for a critical stance in regard to it. He expressly distinguishes his position from liberal theology, which he understands as a theology that uncritically accepts the actual historical process of the modern age, paraphrasing its developments into theological terms without uncovering their questionable features (1972b: 159–61).

At the same time, with all those qualifications, it remains true that an acceptance of modernity in the concrete form of the Enlightenment, of its principles and of the process it set in motion, is the basis of Metz's political theology. He deplores the isolation of the Church from the Enlightenment movement of emancipation and attributes the present crisis of Church authority to that isolation. His purpose in promoting political theology is to bring the Church into a positive relationship with what he calls the Enlightenment process (*Aufklärungsprozess*).

While we may exonerate Metz from the charge of uncritical naivety in his theory of modernity and the Enlightenment, the question still arises of the correctness of his interpretation and, more importantly, of the grounds on which his theory is based. Now, as de Lavalette, a French critic of his theology, remarks, Metz's treatment of history is troubling (1970: 332 n. 23; 343). Although he takes the Enlightenment as a basic theme, he never once discusses the divergent interpretations of so complex a phenomenon. He grossly over-simplifies the emergence of modern subjectivity and the history of modern freedoms. The plural 'freedoms' better indicates the diversity that would emerge from an analysis more concrete than Metz's abstract concept of freedom-history. The interpretation Metz gives, which relates the origin of both subjectivity and political freedom to Christianity, clearly rests upon a pre-understanding drawn from Christian faith. He finds in history what he brings to history. We may well grant the legitimacy of interpreting history from a Christian standpoint, but it still remains indefensible to neglect the different elements involved in complex cultural developments. His failure to give a concrete analysis of the economic, social and political factors makes his thesis on the rise of modern subjectivity and freedom arbitrary. History here becomes the clothing of *a priori* theory or, in other words, a scarcely camouflaged ideology (de Lavalette, 1970: 346).

There are those who would regard Marxism as equally arbitrary and *a priori*, but it is instructive to compare the theology of modernity, which is hardly one step beyond Bossuet in method, though it exploits a different set of prejudices, with historical materialism in its interpretation by Habermas as an empirically falsifiable philosophy of history with practical intent.[10] Marx did not ask the ontological question why is there something rather than nothing, but the historical question why is this existing situation thus and not otherwise. The theoretical task was therefore to explain how the present historical situation came about. He considered the task a scientific, empirical one, though not one implying any separation of fact and value. For him the present situation became theoretically known in the measure in which men and women set about practically working for its transformation. The meaning of history is its possible future to be realized through action. The factual, contingent historical process is uncovered in its constituents and meaning by practice, which in its endeavours to change society comes up against the contradictions of the present social order and the real possibilities these contradictions imply. Historical materialism as a scientific theory of society is thus the theoretical counterpart of the practice of transforming society. It is both practical in intent and itself as theory mediated by practice. It declares itself open to verification or falsification empirically and is thus subject to modification as the situation changes and practice changes with it.

49

The general conclusion Marx arrived at through his study of political economy, a conclusion which then became 'the guiding principle' (Colletti, ed., 1975: 425) of his studies and the reason why his theory is a 'materialism' is stated with lucidity in the Preface to *A Contribution to the Critique of Political Economy*:

In the social production of their existence, men inevitably enter into definite relations, which are independent of their will, namely relations of production appropriate to a given stage in the development of their material forces of production. The totality of these relations of production constitutes the economic structure of society, the real foundation, on which arises a legal and political superstructure and to which correspond definite forms of social consciousness. The mode of production of material life conditions the general process of social, political and intellectual life. It is not the consciousness of men that determines their existence, but their social existence that determines their consciousness (*ibid.*, 425).

Neither Marx nor Engels interpreted the relation between the economic base and the superstructure of forms of social consciousness in a mechanistic, deterministic fashion, but dialectically in a manner that allowed the superstructure to react upon the economic base.

Considering the abstract vagueness and *a priori* remoteness of the theological attempts to interpret modernity, it is hardly surprising that the South American theologies of liberation and some left-wing Christians in Europe have taken over the Marxist analysis of society and the Marxist interpretation of history. Marxist theory does deal with concrete issues and it does relate to practice, namely to social action aimed at transforming society. Why does theology remain in the misty clouds of abstraction, even when talking of modernity? Is it not because it has lost any actual, effective relationship to social practice? However much theologians talk about *praxis*, their theology remains dogmatic in so far as they continue to spin their new theories out of prior, sacrosanct concepts and doctrines, without allowing a genuinely practical mediation of theological theory. For that reason, even political theology has produced no theological theory of the modern world that can withstand a critique made with reference to social reality in history and practice.

3

Faith and social policy

Contemporary political theology in its various forms demands an option for social change. Christian faith, it contends, is only genuine when it includes a commitment to struggle for a transforming liberation of men and women in society. In other words, political theology puts faith into history and in doing so locates it in the politics of emancipatory social change.

It thus establishes an essential link between Christian faith and political liberation. What are the grounds it offers for doing this? There are several.

First, the biblical word of God, the word of revelation, is understood as a word of promise. That is the basic principle of Moltmann's theology of hope. 'The writings in the Old and New Testaments', he writes, 'comprise the history book of God's promises' (1975: 45). This promissory history 'recounts the past in such a way that through it a new future and freedom for the hearers are inaugurated' (*ibid*.). It tells 'the story of the anticipations of God's future in the past and makes what is open, incomplete, and unsatisfied in this past a matter of real concern again' (*ibid*.). Metz agrees with Moltmann that the biblical word is primarily not a word of personal address or of divine self-communication, but a word of promise, announcing the future. It helps here to notice that, in their attitude to the future, there is a contrast between Metz and Moltmann on the one hand and Pannenberg on the other. Pannenberg with his concept of universal history as the comprehensive context for faith and theology sees the future simply as fulfilment. For Metz and Moltmann history is an open experiment, representing a risk, and they conceive the future as promise (Johns, 1976: 102–5). For that reason, their interpretation of the biblical word as a word of promise stresses the imperative it implies to

51

seek the future God pledges by striving for liberation in the present.

Second, in his political theology Metz argues that the key concepts of the biblical message, such as kingdom, covenant, freedom, peace, righteousness and reconciliation, cannot without distortion be privatized, that is, given an individualist interpretation. They are all social concepts. Consequently, a response to the biblical message implies a commitment to their social realization, which is in effect an alignment with a political and social emancipation.

Third, both the prophets and the Gospel are manifestly on the side of the poor and the oppressed. Moltmann puts the familiar observation with the new force it acquires from political awareness:

> If we begin to read the Bible as the book of God's hope, then we will find that it is a highly revolutionary and subversive book. The hope about which it speaks is valid for the hopeless and not for the optimists. It is valid for the poor and not for the rich. It is valid for the downtrodden and the insulted so that they will raise up their heads (1975: 46).

Not surprisingly, the same point is thundered out in the black theology of liberation. James Cone writes:

> There can be no Christian theology which is not identified unreservedly with those who are humiliated and abused. In fact, theology ceases to be a theology of the gospel when it fails to arise out of the community of the oppressed. For it is impossible to speak of the God of Israelite history, who is the God who revealed himself in Jesus Christ, without recognizing that he is the God *of* and *for* those who labor and are heavy laden (1970: 17–18 – Cone's italics).

Finally, there is the conviction etched upon the minds of the Latin American theologians by the realities of the actual situation in which they live: namely, that it is impossible truly to love one's neighbour without engaging in politics. When in a situation of cruel oppression we love our neighbours in a down-to-earth and fearless fashion, where does that practice of love lead us? It led Camillo Torres to resign his priesthood and join guerillas working for a violent revolution. But even if we question that extreme decision, it is difficult to elude all political commitment. If we begin with a simple compassion for the need and misery we immediately see, we shall be led to reflect upon and to try to tackle the causes of that need and misery. Unless we arbitrarily place a limit upon what we are prepared to do, we shall find ourselves concerned about our neighbour's world, his work, his living conditions and resolved to set about changing what is wrong in his social position and environment. Very soon we shall be up against defects and injustices in the legal system, struggling with the destructive effects of the economic system and angry at the stunting of human freedom, the psychic maiming of so many people by the structures of society. Politics means taking a definite stand on practical, public issues. Unless we are prepared to say in the name of Christ to our brother and sister in need, I can help you so far but no further, our Christian love will become political in virtue of its own logic. In short, the Christian practice of love mediates a political interpretation of Christian faith.

But it is here that considerable difficulties arise. How does one pass from faith to the practical decisions of political action? Granted that Christian faith contains a general imperative to work for the liberation of the oppressed, does that mean it is possible to derive a practical political programme from it at any time or place? Since any political programme has to take account of contingent factors, in what manner is faith brought to bear upon these factors and upon the empirical sciences, such as sociology, political science, economics, communications, which study them? Surely, faith of itself relates us to the transcendent, both to the transcendent God and his salvation as transcendent gift. That would seem to imply that faith and our unity in the faith stand above our political conflicts. Is it, then, not possible for those who are one in the Christian faith to differ in their understanding of social reality and history and in their decisions for or against particular political policies and actions? On the other hand, if there is no distinctively Christian contribution to political decision and action, then political theology is wrong in giving a political interpretation to faith and in placing faith and its expression in the midst of the movement for political emancipation. It would also be difficult to escape Marx's critique of religion as unreal consolation, because faith would then be disengaged from concrete social existence.

The difficulty, in short, is to retain the transcendence of faith and of the community of faith and to refuse to identify these with a particular political programme or party, while at the same time relating faith positively and effectively to the work of human liberation in this world. Or, are we here simply confronting a contradiction? How great at least is the difficulty is shown by the criticism of Metz's position from both Right and Left. From the Right he has been accused of a new integralism, understanding integralism as the effort to explain or master social and political reality exclusively by faith and the action of the Church. From the Left his theology has been dubbed academic and lacking in critical insight, and he has been rebuked above all for not applying the political imperatives he finds in the Gospel to the hierarchical Church itself in a concrete fashion (Johns, 1976: 167–70).

Segundo in *The Liberation of Theology* endeavours to solve the problem of faith and social action by exploiting a distinction between faith and ideology, using the term 'ideology' in a good sense. By 'ideology' he means 'the system of goals and means that serves as the necessary backdrop for any human option or line of action' (1977: 102). He goes on to explain: 'Real life for a human being presupposes a nonempirical choice of some ideal that one presumes will be satisfying. It is this ideal, chosen ahead of time by nonempirical standards, that organizes and gives direction to the means and ends used to attain it. Those means and ends are what we have been calling ideology here' (*ibid.*, 104). In other words, we are motivated by faith, which is the nonempirical choice of an ideal, and the result in our concrete situation is an ideology, namely an organized system of ends and means. Faith and ideology are inextricably intermingled and yet to be clearly distinguished from each other. Faith is recognized 'in the fact that it claims to possess an *objectively* absolute value. In his faith a person supposedly comes in contact with an objective font of total truth' (*ibid.*, 107 – Segundo's italics). But this encounter

takes place in and through a process of ideological searching and has immediate ideological consequences. No one links up with absolute truth except in an effort to give truth and meaning to one's own life. There is an *ideological* intention at work. But it does seem that the fact of faith does relativize any and every particular ideology, even though it certainly does not relativize the general need for ideologies in orienting one's life (*ibid.* – Segundo's italics).

For that reason, faith without ideologies is a dead faith. Faith makes no sense unless it leads us to give direction to our lives or, in other words, leads to an ideology. At the same time, that direction or ideology is relativized by faith, so that, if the ideology becomes inoperative, my faith leads me to change it.

What, then, does the Christian faith say to me in the concrete? What is its truth content? Nothing (*ibid.* 108). To make his meaning clear, Segundo puts the point also in another way. 'If someone were to ask me', he writes, 'what I have derived from my faith-inspired encounter as a clear-cut, absolute truth that can validly give orientation to my concrete life, then my honest response should be: nothing' (*ibid.*). Does faith, then, have any objective meaning, once we have discarded the ideological element? Here Segundo introduces a distinction he takes from Gregory Bateson's *Steps to an Ecology of Mind* between proto-learning and deutero-learning, that is, between simple learning and learning to learn. What we have in the Bible is a series of faith encounters, each bound up with a specific and changing context, each therefore embodied in a particular ideology. But through that historical process people learned how to learn. Segundo writes:

We can say without fear of error that the ideologies present in Scripture belong to the first level. They are responses learned vis-à-vis specific historical situations. Faith, by contrast, is the total process to which man submits, a process of learning in and through ideologies how to create the ideologies needed to handle new and unforeseen situations in history (*ibid.*, 120).

Deutero-learning, to which faith belongs, has its own proper content, but that content is not ideological, but essentially methodological (*ibid.*, 109). Consequently:

Faith, then, is not a universal, atemporal, pithy body of content summing up divine revelation once the latter has been divested of ideologies, on the contrary, it is maturity by way of ideologies, the possibility of fully and conscientiously carrying out the ideological task on which the real-life liberation of human beings depends (*ibid.*, 122).

In that fashion Segundo tries to reconcile the absoluteness of faith with the relativity of politics. He begins from a concern with the way the faith of Christians is frequently emptied of its political force against the established order, its potential as a protest neutralized, by the plea that Christian faith is not an ideology and must therefore be kept free from any political involvement. What is his solution? It consists in two linked assertions. The first is that faith in general is the free choice of some value as the centre of one's whole life and therefore as absolute. In principle the absolutization is subjective and free. The value as absolute cannot be empirically grounded or rationally demonstrated; its absoluteness arises from a free decision. The second assertion is that the Christian option 'does not absolutize a value or a doctrine but rather an educational process dealing with values' (*ibid.*, 178). Divine revelation is a deutero-learning process, and so faith cannot be reduced to a specific content. Dogmas simply define 'the boundaries within which we can say that we are still operating inside the same educational tradition' (*ibid.*, 180). For Christians, however, the absolute value is not just subjective, because in this case 'we absolutize one objective tradition among many possible traditions' (*ibid.*). Faith is thus embodied in the successive ideologies of the tradition. It is not itself an ideology, but without ideologies it would be dead.

Apart from a different use of the word 'ideology', Segundo's solution reminds one of the distinction I have previously mentioned as made by Richardson between teleological and procedural values. What Richardson calls a political as distinct from a nonpolitical society respects the plurality of teleological values. In doing so, it adopts and institutionalizes a set of procedural values, enabling government as a process to be through the coming together of a multitude of wills in a cowilling. The faith of a political community is not tied to any particular religious content, but is faith in a transcendent higher principle that relativizes all specific contents.

Thus faith for both Segundo and Richardson has not of itself a particular objective content, but relativizes all such contents. Segundo's deutero-learning process corresponds to Richardson's procedural values.[11]

I personally doubt whether a solution to the question how to

relate faith as absolute and transcendent with contingent political policy and action can be found by making a dichotomy
between teleological and procedural values or between proto-
learning and deutero-learning. The procedural values of a pluralist society, if they are not just temporary expedients,
originate in and continue to imply a set of truths and values
concerning the human condition and human destiny.
Richardson to some extent recognizes this in declaring that the
faith of a political community excludes all immanentalistic
forms of religion. At the same time, he considers – without sufficient reason I think – that people with divergent views of
human happiness and fulfilment and thus of ultimate goals
and values can agree on procedural values alone, compromise
their differences and interact politically. The agreement he
asks for has in my opinion more presuppositions than he is
prepared to admit. Likewise, deutero-learning is determined
in its character and form by the proto-learning to which it is related. Learning to learn mathematics is not the same type of activity as learning to learn moral values.

We cannot avoid, I should argue, examining the content of
the Christian tradition and asking how that content is related
to the political enterprise in general and to individual political
policies and actions in particular. The Christian tradition is
indeed a complex reality, subject to wide-ranging changes and
containing much that is clearly relative. But for those who are
Christians it also has a continuity, an identity in change. It is a
mistake to suppose that one can clearly demarcate faith in its
transcendent absoluteness from its contingent, historical
embodiment. Faith for human beings is available and present
only as mediated through historically relative language, symbols, events and institutions. But the relativity of these media
does not mean that they are dispensable or replaceable features of faith. They share in the absoluteness of faith, in so far
as they are at a particular time and place the indispensable,
irreplaceable form of faith. A comparison may help here.
There is a difference between clothes and the body as expressive media of the human self. Clothes, which can be changed at
any time, correspond to the always dispensable elements of
the tradition, which easily admit great variety. The body,
though it too constantly changes, shares the permanence of

the self, because in its changing it is unceasingly moulded so as to remain within the identity of that self. Likewise, the essential features of a religious tradition, though they change, are continually governed in their changing by the absolute focus of its faith. For that reason, the Christian tradition does have an objective content that permanently excludes other contents. To take a simple example, it excludes any view that denies the essential equality of human beings, despite changing formulations of its positive conception of humanness. This exclusivity of the Christian tradition does not necessitate any denial that there are other traditions that mediate a genuinely transcendent faith.

We are right, therefore, to ask questions about politics and the Christian tradition, as that tradition has revealed its general thrust, its potentialities and implications, down through the centuries of its history. Such an investigation does, however, presuppose a preliminary question: What kind of content does the Christian tradition give us? A body of general principles? A set of practical precepts? An evaluative account of what is going on in history? A way of looking at experience as a whole? An interpretation of fundamental elements of human existence? A symbolic world-view or mythical cosmology? Faith is never a naked adherence to the transcendent. Faith meets the presence of the transcendent through one or other of the cultural forms I have mentioned.

To some extent, what I am saying does correspond to Segundo's contention that faith is so inextricably bound up with ideology that without ideology it is dead. There is, however, a difference. His use of the term 'ideology' shows that he makes a sharper distinction between faith and its objective content and allows a greater relativity of that content than I am prepared to admit. For me the objective content of faith participates in its permanence. Furthermore, for Segundo ideology includes and, I should say, confuses the concrete embodiment of an ideal on the one hand and the choice of means and ends in a social policy adapted to a particular situation on the other. But the latter, namely practical action in a contingent context, is relative in a sense in which the former, namely the objective content of a faith, is not.

There are in fact two distinct but related problems here. The first is the relation between the absoluteness of faith and the relativity of its objective content as a determinate normative account of human existence. The second is the relation between that normative account as theory and the practical decisions called for by action in changing situations. How does one pass from the general Christian understanding of human existence to concrete political commands? A long-standing complaint against the Churches is that they evade their political responsibility by simply repeating vague general principles without clearly stating the Christian's political obligation in the actual situation. But does the content of Christian faith allow one to derive a precise political command from it?

Metz, in answering that last question, stresses that political theology is only indirectly linked to action, namely through a political ethic. Political theology for him is eschatological theology, that is, its subject-matter is eschatology, understood as the ultimate outcome of history. Any immediate translation of eschatology into politics he rejects as a naked ideologizing of politics and the ruin of eschatology. Eschatological statements refer to history as a whole, the final end of which God reserves to himself. That is Metz's well-known teaching on the eschatological reserve or proviso. History as a whole can never be the source of maxims for political action and can never become the content of political policy, because when eschatologically interpreted, history as a whole has no immediate political subject. Whenever a party, group, nation or class understands itself as the direct subject of total history, the result is a totalitarian political ideology.

What, then, is the relation between political theology and the political ethics which joins it to action? Metz distinguishes between an ethics of order and an ethics of change. The modern situation demands an ethics of change. Analytical reflection and reasoning are insufficient for an ethics of change, because that ethics has to confront the question of the historical foundations of a society taken in its entirety. To handle that question it must make use of procedures of interpretation, namely a hermeneutic. It is in this context that Metz defines political theology as the specifically Christian hermeneutic implied by political ethics as an ethics of change (1969b: 282).

Metz goes on to acknowledge that such an understanding of political theology does not solve the further problem of the relation between theory and practice in theology. Hermeneutical procedures are themselves tied to practice, because they cannot be confined to elucidating the conditions and horizon of interpretation in a particular situation, but have to handle the question of changes in those very conditions and horizon of understanding. The theory–practice dialectic, therefore, calls for a new relationship between dogmatics and ethics. Ethics can no longer be taken as the mere application of dogmatics. Metz, however, leaves the problem, noting that it is difficult to set forth a positive alternative without falling into an opposite onesidedness (1969b: 283–4).

Hugo Assmann, from the standpoint of a theology of liberation, considers Metz's distinction between political ethics and political theology a 'fundamental error', because it misconceives the theory–practice relationship and abandons the concrete context of practice (Bauer, 1976: 225; Johns, 1976: 168). The full content of that kind of objection is subtly analysed by Xhaufflaire in his sympathetic study of Metz, where he writes of a theoretical capitulation of political theology (1972: 132–40). Because Metz does not allow any political theory to handle satisfactorily the question of the meaning and subject of history, he cannot provide any theoretical mediation of practice. Instead, he has to motivate practice ethically, not theoretically. For Xhaufflaire the only genuine possibility for the development of political theology is the production within theology itself of theoretical, explanatory accounts of the conditions of freedom and oppression. Using its own presuppositions, theology has to process information from other sciences to produce such theologico-political theories. The political misery of present-day theology comes from the fact that, ever since theology has been unwilling to serve as a mere legitimation of ecclesiastical authority, it has become devoid of any positive significance on the political level. Unlike conservative theologies, the theologies coming from a Church newly aware of itself as at the service of the poor and oppressed have so far proved themselves incapable of producing a coherent political theory. Hence, theology tries in a nonpolitical fashion to legitimate the political interventions it advocates. By that very fact its political interventions remain politically incoherent, voluntarist and baldly opportunist.

The constant appeal to practice in recent theology is just an excuse for a lack of theory. The idea of a spontaneous *ortho-praxis* is a myth. Recourse is had to ethical inspiration to cover over the absence of theoretical criteria for action. But where there is a situation of oppression, a practice inspired by an ethics of change comes both too early and too late. Too early: because it comes without the work of analysis necessary to make it adequate and effectual in dealing with the oppression. Too late: because theory is thereby led to constitute itself in relation to ethical rather than political practice and is not therefore, as it should be, a theoretical discourse arising out of a real emancipatory practice.

The gist, then, of Xhaufflaire's contentions as I understand them is that the dialectical relationship between theory and practice renders unnecessary and indeed mistaken the insertion of ethics as a distinct moment. Theory gives an evaluative analysis of the concrete situation, which thus provides the criteria needed to guide practice. Practice, in its turn, as an internal factor in the formation of theory, provides the insights needed to develop, modify and correct theory. The appeal to ethics gets a bad press from some who do not share Xhaufflaire's view of the theoretical task of theology in relation to politics. Fierro contrasts contemporary political theologies with what he calls 'Christendom theology', described as 'primarily an ethics'. He continues:

It had to do with the ethico-political consequences of dogma, with Christian love and Christian action as consequences of faith; but it did not have to do with the faith itself. It was political theology insofar as it embodied a social morality based on dogma and logically flowing from it. It presupposed a separation between dogmatic theology and moral theology, which today is regarded as 'ideology' in the worst sense of the term (1977: 72–3).

Here, in the case of Fierro, unlike Xhaufflaire, the rejection of the method of deriving ethical consequences from prior doctrine is taken as implying there is no Christian or theologically based social theory. Fierro writes:

Present-day theology has given up the idea of fashioning a model

Christian society. It holds no preconceived idea as to what the social order ought to be like, much less some picture of a social order shaped by the gospel politics. There is simply the public and critical praxis of Christians. This praxis is not just a consequence of the faith. Rather, it is intrinsic to the faith as a factor that sustains and determines its meaning (*ibid.*, 75).

The passage seems to assume that any Christian social theory will consist of preconceived ideas.

The Protestant theologian Dorothee Sölle emphatically states the same exclusion of a specifically Christian political programme or theory:

Furthermore, political theology is not an attempt to develop a concrete political program from faith, nor is it another type of Social Gospel in which praxis simply swallows up theory. There are no specifically Christian solutions to world problems for which a political theology would have to develop the theory (1974: 59).

What, then, is political theology? She answers:

Political theology is rather a theological hermeneutic, which, in distinction from a theology that interprets reality from an ontological or existentialist point of view, holds open an horizon of interpretation in which politics is understood as the comprehensive and decisive sphere in which Christian truth should become praxis (*ibid.*).

A simple example makes clear what she means by a political hermeneutic. Writing of the Christian truth, 'God loves you!', she says:

Because all reality is worldly and inherently social, even this statement must be interpreted politically; it has meaning only when it intends the transformation of the status quo. Suppose this is addressed to a man who has lived for fifteen years in the slums of our cities. The contempt that he has suffered makes such a statement incredible to him and leaves him unable to believe in the love of God (*ibid.*, 67–8).

There seems to me to be a confusion here between the content of the statement and the conditions of its credibility. The difficulty or impossibility of its acceptance by a socially oppressed individual does not necessarily imply that its content concerns political liberation. Such liberation may be simply the prior condition for the acceptance of a higher truth. At the end of her little book, *Political Theology*, Sölle gives a more detailed political interpretation of sin and forgiveness.

But what is the Christian Gospel that a political interpret-ation of it is considered appropriate? According to Sölle, from the Gospel political theology 'obtains the nonderivable prom-ise and the demand for peace, freedom and justice for all people' (*ibid.*, 76). She goes on to insist, however, that this truth of Christ exists only as concrete realization. Theory and practice can be understood only in their unity, which means that truth is something we make true. Thus:

That God loves all of us and each and every individual is a universal theological truth, which without translation becomes the universal lie. The translation of this proposition is world-transforming praxis. It needs a degree of concreteness, without which it remains empty. But at the same time this proposition necessarily transcends every concrete manifestation and has neither been exhausted nor rendered invalid in its translations. We have in it a greater claim than is fulfilled at any given time, a deeper want than is satisfied (*ibid.*, 107).

The conclusion, then, would seem to be that Christian truth is a gospel of liberation, though apparently in the most general terms, which do not allow the formation of a Christian social theory. Nevertheless, the Gospel is to be understood politi-cally and made both concrete and credible by an emancipatory practice. All the same, it cannot be translated politically without remainder. It always transcends every particular reali-zation; there is always something more, yet to be satisfied.

Fierro draws a parallel between negative theology in general and political theology, seeing political theology as negative theology, in so far as there is 'the total absence of positive as-sertions dealing with any strict knowledge of social reality or with the conditions surrounding its possible alteration' (1977: 254). Christians will not find out what they must do in a situ-ation by exegetical or theological discussions, but by a rational and scientific analysis of the situation, using the concepts of social theory. He declares roundly: 'There is no Christian social theory, no Christian praxis, no Christian politics' (*ibid.*, 255).

What the Gospel gives is a different order, namely a set of regulatory ideas, a comprehensive horizon, symbols that allude to what is concrete and given in experience, but at the same time transcend the given.

The attempt to discover what political theology says about the relation between faith and social policy has led us on a long and complicated journey. Political theology we have found speaks with confused and conflicting voices on the question of the Christian contribution to politics. The predominant opinion, though elaborated and grounded in varying ways, denies any specifically Christian social theory or social practice. There is a firm rejection of any attempt to re-establish a Christian order of society. Faith or the Gospel is seen as operative on a higher level than social theory or concrete political practice. Some want to qualify that negative stance. Segundo, while keeping faith itself free from political content, sees it as inseparably bound up with a succession of ideologies of a Christian character. Again, for Metz Christian faith does provide an account of history as a whole in terms of an eschatological hope and with specific liberating memories, but no political programme can be directly derived from that objective content, which needs political ethics to connect it with practice. The appeal to ethics is an attempt to jump over the gap left empty by the absence of social theory. Of the authors examined only Xhaufflaire is prepared to undertake the task of producing a social theory on the terrain of theology.

The confused hesitancy of political theology about the Christian contribution to political policy and action is the reflection, in my opinion, of the lack of any real and effective functional relationship between Christian institutions and society as at present organized. Christian talk on politics has become unreal, stripped of both theory and programme, because it is the free-ranging speech of the disengaged. This is not to deny the personal commitment of Christian individuals and groups. But that commitment remains an essentially private affair. The Christian communities as organized communities stay uncommitted in practice, even though hortatory generalities upon social matters circulate among their members. They do so, because they are no longer a functioning part of political society. Where Church authorities retain fragments of the real power they exercised in the past, it is now used as pressure to preserve ecclesiastical institutions for their own sake. Meanwhile, the Christian people accept a political pluralism within their Christian communities of a kind that effectively neutralizes any political significance the Christian faith might have. Political theology has not succeeded in counteracting that neutralization, because it continues to reify the Christian tradition and interpret the transcendent quality of faith in an unreal and abstract fashion.

I consider the Christian tradition as reified when the fact is lost sight of that the primary reality in question is a community of people. (The total Christian community, it should be noted, is a community of communities, that is, a complex network of communities with different degrees of interrelationship.) The Christian tradition is the common meaning shared by those who call themselves Christians and who acknowledge one another as Christians. As a community of real people, past and present, the Christian community has gone through many vicissitudes, with quarrels, divisions and reconciliations, but, despite blurred boundaries and variable unity, it is a recognizable group within history. The common meaning it shares, namely its tradition, has also had its ups and downs.

Elements with a good claim to represent its original inspiration and authentic meaning have become intermingled with what were later denounced with some reason as errors and corruptions. The days of first innocence when the Christian tradition could be accepted uncritically have long past. The common meaning of the Christian community has undergone many changes, some of which constitute a cumulative development, others a distortion and process of decline. Common meaning is always an achievement. Hence, the degree in which meaning has been shared among Christians has differed widely from time to time and from place to place. Nevertheless, the Christian tradition is still living as long as a group of people, calling themselves Christians, share a common understanding and a common set of judgements with some claim to continuity with the Christian past.

Now, that this Christian tradition or common meaning shared by the Christian people has a content that is relevant to politics and can originate political theories and policy and action is surely clear from the fact that it has continually done so in the past. A new situation has undoubtedly arisen in modern times. There is a new distinction between society and the State. There is a new consciousness of freedom, which excludes any authoritative imposition of political policy and action and demands that even within the Christian Church any political stance must be reached through open discussion and consensus, with the participation of all the members. There is the new recognition of the positive value of pluralism, obliging any society that respects the dignity and freedom of its members to allow for a plurality of views even on fundamental issues, so that political unity is by compromise not by suppression of dissent. There is the rise of the social sciences, requiring that political policy and action should take account of the empirical data as scientifically gathered, interpreted or explained. All these factors, constitutive of a new situation, certainly demand a major change in Christian political theories, policy and action, but they in no way imply that there is no longer any distinctively Christian contribution to politics. The attempt to exclude that rests not upon a consideration of the concrete actuality of the Christian tradition, but upon a narrow and abstract concept of faith.

Faith's relation to transcendent reality is distilled from all changing elements. But this is to deprive faith of its rich substance. Faith in the concrete, when taken objectively, is the meaning a tradition actually has here and now for a person or community. My Christian faith is the meaning the Christian tradition actually has for me. The Christian faith of a particular Christian community is the configuration of elements from the Christian tradition actually operative as the common meaning of that community. Taken in that sense, the Christian faith embraces a whole way of life, because the meanings actualized by faith are primarily present in human actions. Faith thus constitutes a pattern of meaningful human actions; it is essentially a form of practice, though the meanings constitutive of Christian actions are formulated as beliefs.

The meanings, which thus constitute faith as a way of life and are articulated as beliefs, are subject to change. Faith as a pattern or orientation of human actions exists only in and through changing elements. Since there is continuity, that is, identity-in-change, in Christian faith, there must indeed be some invariant factors shaping the changing actions and meanings into a recognizably identical pattern or direction. But every attempt to isolate and formulate the invariant elements is relative and changing; in other words, every attempted delineation of the essence or permanent structure of Christian faith becomes dated, because it is itself only an instance of changing human action as shaped by the underlying, not directly accessible prototype.

The individual meanings, going to make up the Christian way of life at a particular time and forming therefore part of the content of Christian faith at that time, do not merely change; they suffer rejection as inadequate or even false. To give two examples. The denial of religious freedom was part of the Christian way of life in past centuries. The denial was lived out in action; it was formulated in teaching and decrees; it was incorporated in the institutions of Church and State. To say that it was not part of the Christian faith is to evade reality with an abstraction. Again, the Christian faith, understood as the common meaning present in the Christian community as its self-understanding, has long included a concept of woman that subordinates women to men. The concept is present already in the Bible; it is further elaborated in the Fathers of the Church and in the medieval and modern theologians; it has been institutionalized in the Church; it has deeply affected both the doctrinal and the devotional life of Christians. Nevertheless, that concept is now widely rejected by Christians and actively combated in feminist theology.

In both these instances, the individual element of meaning, later recognized as false, formed in its day part of a whole, namely of a way of life, a faith, which we acknowledge as genuinely though imperfectly Christian. The rejected elements were in the past vehicles of Christian values, which they both conveyed and distorted. The patristic concept of the virgin was simultaneously an ideal and a distortion. It helps here to remember that Christian meanings are primarily located in actions. The ambiguity of human actions is somehow easier to accept than the ambiguity of concepts and propositions.

The two examples are also instances that imply a political stance on the part of the Christian community. The fact that Christians now reject and deplore the past political stance of their tradition against religious freedom and the emancipation of women should not lead them to avoid a political commitment for the future. Instead, they should adopt a new political stance for religious freedom and the liberation of women on the grounds that this is what the Christian faith as the present actualization of the common meaning within the Christian community demands today.

There is no unalloyed relation to God as transcendent reality. The Christian way of life is a religious faith because it is grounded upon and open to the transcendent. But that transcendent reality is reached only in and through the life of the community and the common meanings constitutive of that life. God is the reality whose immanent presence within the life of the community is experienced as the ground or ultimate basis of its existence and whose all-encompassing mystery is experienced as disclosing the limits of all our actions, meanings and strivings as human and finite and therefore subject to change, corruption and error. But one cannot isolate the experience of the limiting reality, namely of the transcendent, from the way of life, the orientation of which opens it out upon the limit. It is only because the transcendent is experienced as immanent within the life of the community that the communal is experienced as bounded by the transcendent.

More concretely, it is only when Christians as Christians engage in politics that they experience the transcendent reality of God as limiting the political. Otherwise their talk of the limits of politics is merely an expression of dissatisfaction with a particular kind of politics rather than a religious experience of the finitude of the political as limited by the transcendent.

There is a great fear that if a distinctively Christian contribution to political theory, policy and action were allowed, the transcendence of faith and its object would be denied and politics given an absolute value. But if one ignores the immanence of transcendent reality in history and keeps God as an isolated reality, reached by faith outside history and at a distance from the world, the world and history become an autonomous totality and thus virtually absolute. Only the immanence of the transcendent in history prevents the monolithic totalization of society, which is feared. Christians must enter into every sphere of human life, social, political and cultural, and establish there a Christian way of life, if they are to bring to each sphere that experience of its finitude which comes only by experiencing that particular sphere of life within the all-encompassing reality of God.

Besides an abstract concept of faith that makes it an unchanging relation to an unchanging object, a specifically Christian contribution to politics is blocked by a failure to appreciate the distinctive rationality appropriate to practical questions. (I am using 'practical' not in the sense of 'useful' or 'feasible', but as referring to norms and values.) There is the mistaken supposition that anything done or proposed in the name of Christian faith has to have permanence and certainty as God's truth. Even if we allow, which I do not, that such permanence and certainty are available on the doctrinal level, it is doubly mistaken to seek it on the level of practical decisions. No practical question, as Aristotle saw (1966: 27–8), can ever be resolved with the certitude of abstract theory. When a group of Christians, for example, decide that their Christian principles demand that they work for socialism in their particular concrete situation, that decision, even when validated as right, does not make socialism an unchanging truth. What further confuses in this matter is the assumption that anything binding upon Christians as Christians must be imposed upon them by authority, whether this authority is conceived as the hierarchical Church or the Bible. But, again, practical decisions of their nature are validated as right only by an unconstrained discussion among all those actually involved in the concrete situation.

I am drawing here upon the ideas of Habermas, who has done much to clarify the relation between theory and practice. Some of the distinctions he makes are helpful, I think, in relating Christian faith to political policy and action. His own perspective is indeed very different. He is concerned with emancipation as an interest constitutive of a particular mode of knowledge, and his endeavour is to ground that emancipatory interest through an analysis of the structure of communication and its normative basis. I want to consider his account of emancipation and his theory of communication for their own sake in the next chapter. Meanwhile, I shall merely anticipate some points as relevant to my present theme.

Habermas sets out to show the intrinsic relation between knowledge and what he terms 'human interests'. He does not

understand the interests psychologically, but transcenden-
tally as deep-seated invariants constituting the *a priori* structure of human knowing. He relates each interest to an
essential formative element of society. The interests are thus
linked with social media, because Habermas refuses to posit
any transcendental subject distinct from the empirical, naturally generated and socially formed subjects. The subject,
therefore, is properly the species as reproducing itself under
cultural conditions.

He distinguishes three interests as constituting three modes
of knowledge. They are: the technical interest, which grounds
the information that gives us technical control and is related to
the social medium of work; the practical interest, which lies
behind the interpretative knowledge of a common tradition,
required for human action and communication, and is related
to the social medium of language; the emancipatory interest,
which makes possible what he calls 'critique', namely knowledge that takes the form of analyses freeing a person from reified social powers, that is, from unanalysed relations of
oppression and dependence and is thus related to the social
medium of power (1972b: 313).

The emancipatory interest is in a different class from the
other two interests, because of the way it is bound up with the
process of self-reflection. The technical and practical interests
are not conscious factors in the method of the first two modes
of knowledge. The scientist or the interpreter of tradition need
not be consciously pursuing technical control or social action.
The interests are not themselves part of the knowledge they
ground. They are brought to light only by self-reflection, and
the first two kinds of knowledge can be found where there is
not yet self-reflection. It is only in self-reflection that the subject becomes transparent to itself. Emancipation, however,
implies such self-reflection, being a coming of the subject to
self-transparency coincides with the subject's movement
towards autonomy and responsibility. For that reason, the
emancipatory interest, unlike the other two cognitive
interests, is operative as a conscious orientation. The conscious movement of the subject in self-reflection towards a
self-transparent autonomy and responsibility is identical with
the coming to an emancipatory knowledge that frees it from

unrecognized dependencies. The interest in emancipation thus becomes actual as a conscious orientation in the knowledge given in self-reflection. Consequently, critique, the third mode of knowledge, is said by Habermas to be the unity of knowledge and interest. The interest is activated to the extent that the emancipatory self-knowledge, fulfilling it, is achieved (1972b: 195–8; 1974a: 9).

In his further account of self-reflection, which is thus identically emancipatory interest and knowledge, Habermas uses Freud's psychoanalysis as a model. According to him, Freud redirected deviant processes of self-formation by therapeutically guided self-reflection. But self-reflection is operative as critique in psychoanalysis only because of a unique combination of causal explanation and interpretative understanding. The analyst's interpretation has explanatory power because he draws upon a causal explanation of the repression of meaning. Psychoanalysis, therefore, offers a special kind of hermeneutic understanding, appropriate to the systematically distorted communication of a neurotic, namely explanatory understanding. Explanatory understanding is an interpretation made possible through reference to a causal explanation of a communication otherwise uninterpretable on account of systematic distortion. The model of explanatory understanding is applied by Habermas to critique or emancipatory knowledge generally. Critique of ideology is a process of emancipatory self-reflection, but for it to produce its critical interpretations, which uncover repressed structures of domination and dependence and make people conscious of the objective position they occupy in an unfree society, it must draw upon a critical theory of society, which provides a causal explanation of the present situation. Only in that way does critique become a process of explanatory understanding, and only through an explanatory understanding can the ideologically distorted communication within society be correctly interpreted.

Habermas, therefore, distinguishes two levels in critique or emancipatory knowledge. First, there is the formation and development of critical theories. The claim of these to be true has to be justified in scientific discourse. Second, there is the very process of self-reflection as the explanatory interpretations, enlightening people concerning their objective situation within society and thus freeing them from unrecognized dependencies. The knowledge given in self-reflection is self-authenticating in as much as it is validated when people recognize themselves in the interpretations offered and come to a consciousness of their social reality. Processes of self-reflection can be initiated and fostered in groups.

Distinct from both the production of critical theories and the processes of self-reflection is political action with the practical decisions it implies.

Habermas is clear in affirming that no theory of itself can legitimate such decisions:

Decisions for the political struggle cannot at the outset be justified theoretically and then be carried out organizationally. The sole possible justification at this level is consensus, aimed at in practical discourse, among the participants, who, in the consciousness of their common interests and their knowledge of the circumstances, of the predictable consequences and secondary consequences, are the only ones who can know what risks they are willing to undergo, and with what expectations. There can be no theory which at the outset can assure a world-historical mission in return for the potential sacrifices (1974a: 33).

Enlightenment through self-reflection enables one to act politically in a rational manner in decisions reached in practical discourse, whereas those ensnared in ideology are incapable of rationally clarifying practical questions. But political actions cannot be legitimated by theory, but by prudent decisions, and 'a political struggle can only be legitimately conducted under the precondition that all decisions of consequence will depend on the practical discourse of the participants – here too, and especially here, there is no privileged access to truth' (*ibid.*, 34).

As I have said, I find the analysis of Habermas helpful in clarifying the confused discussion about the relation of Christian faith to social policy and action.

The Christian faith as a way of life comes under the second mode of knowledge, namely knowledge operative within intersubjective communication and grounded upon a practical (that is, concerned with norms and values) interest. In other words, the Christian faith offers a common tradition or set of interpretations, which makes it possible for people to orient their actions through symbolic interaction and mutual understanding. The second mode of knowledge becomes methodical in the historical and hermeneutic disciplines. As methodically elaborated the Christian faith becomes theology, which is an historical and hermeneutical discipline as usually practised and developed.

But the Christian faith as a form of life is an historical reality and therefore subject to corruption, in which its common meanings are ideologically distorted through the structures of unfreedom in human society. The question, then, arises whether critique or emancipatory self-reflection is an element intrinsic to Christian faith itself or the Christian faith is simply the object, not the agent, of such self-reflection. This has been a troublesome question since the Enlightenment. There are those who hold that a critique of ideology completely dissolves Christian faith as a way of life. For those who reject that extreme position, the question still remains, Is critical self-reflection an intrinsic moment within faith itself or is it a critique of faith from an independent reason?

Those for whom Christian faith is critique as well as tradition, subversive of forms of life as well as constructive, urge the need for a critical theology alongside the usual historical and hermeneutical varieties. Such a critical theology will have two tasks: the formation and development of a critical theory of society and history, so as to provide a causal explanation of the present situation; and the initiating and fostering of the process of critical self-reflection within the Christian community. If a critical theory of society and history produced by theology is to have an emancipatory function and provide the causal explanation self-reflection needs in order to offer an explanatory interpretation of people's actual situation in the unfree society of the present, it must arise from an investigation of the empirical data, past and present. In that sense, it must be an empirically falsifiable theory, like historical materialism, which is the Marxist critical theory. The Marxist investigation refuses the positivist separation of fact and value, and is therefore a value-impregnated investigation. We might well ask, therefore, whether an investigation impregnated with Christian values might not produce a different critical theory from that of Marx or, at least, notably modify his. Cannot the values enshrined in the historical myths of Christians find new expression in a critical theory of history and society?

Even were there – which there is not – a critical theology producing critical theories and promoting processes of self-reflection, it would still remain true that political action cannot be legitimated by theology, but only by a consensus reached through unconstrained discussion among those involved. A recognition of this would show that much of the discussion about faith and political action rests upon a mistaken assumption. It seeks a kind of legitimation for practical action that is simply unavailable. Meanwhile, the true source of legitimation for Christian political action is neglected.

An effective political action of Christians is impeded, I suggest, by an inadequate model of the Christian community, which distinguishes, on the one hand, the official, institutional Church, considered as commissioned only for matters of revelation or supernatural salvation and, on the other hand, private individual Christians (with unofficial groups classified as private), who are said to have a directly political mission as Christian lay people. What is missing is the concept of a broadly based, pluralistic, democratically functioning and critically conscious public opinion within the Church, through which Christians generally may develop a consensus in regard to political policy and action. In the nature of the case there will always be differences, necessitating compromise and mutual tolerance, but it is not too much to suppose that a public opinion formed among Christians in a discussion free from domination and constraint would reach sufficient agreement on key issues for effective participation in emancipatory political policy and action.

A major task of political theology is to insist on the creation of this dimension, at present largely absent, within the life of the Churches. Unfortunately, in a strong reaction against the heteronomous Christian politics of the past, political theology manifests a tendency to leave faith as transcendent, soaring above the political sphere in eschatological flight, rather than making it enter more deeply than ever into political reality through a newly found self-reflective autonomy and responsibility of critically conscious Christians.

4

Freedom of discourse and the authority of tradition

Much discussion has been going on in Germany concerning the place of theology among the sciences. The discussion has institutional implications because the position of theology in State universities is in question. A notable contribution to the argument on behalf of theology is Wolfhart Pannenberg's recent *Theology and the Philosophy of Science* (1976). Unfortunately, here we meet the usual difficulty about the translation of *Wissenschaft* and its derivatives. Unlike the English term 'science', *Wissenschaft* refers to any methodically organized knowledge and therefore to all branches of disciplined inquiry, the social as well as the natural sciences, the humanities as well as experimental forms of inquiry. Hence *Wissenschaftstheorie* (Pannenberg's German title is *Wissenschaftstheorie und Theologie*) is much wider than 'philosophy of science', and embraces all the theoretical discussions concerning the status, method and mutual relationship of the whole range of academic disciplines. The question about theology in this context is whether theology is a methodically organized body of knowledge, with intelligible truth claims, which can be critically tested. The answer offered by Pannenberg is that theology to fulfil these requirements, becomes the theology of religion. By the theology of religion he means the science of religion (*Religionswissenschaft*, usually rendered in English as the history of religions), but transformed, so that it investigates the truth claims of religions concerning the self-revelation in them of a divine reality. Such a transformed science of religion will be a science of God, that is, a theology that establishes a knowledge of God from an investigation of religion in its various forms. Pannenberg then sees the theology of Christianity as a branch of the theology of religion. Just as the theology

of religion transforms the history of religions by an examination of the truth claims of the religions concerning the communication of divine reality, so the theology of Christianity
raises Church history and the account of Christian origins into
a theology by including an investigation of the truth of Christian claims concerning the divine action (Cobb and Hodgson,
1977).

Despite the impression given by the English title of his
book, Pannenberg is preoccupied with the place of theology
among the *Geisteswissenschaften* or human sciences rather than
with its relation to the natural sciences, though he does
deplore the sharp division between the two groups of disciplines as mistaken. His account of theology as a science continues his previous work on hermeneutics and history. Both of
these related activities of interpretation require, according to
him, the horizon of universal history. Hermeneutics he conceives as the methodical understanding of meaning, bridging
the gap between the world of the text and the world of the
interpreter. It demands for its understanding of partial meanings the anticipation of total meaning as this is given in universal history. Likewise, historical investigation, concerned with
the relation between texts and the events to which they refer,
must call upon an imaginative projection of the whole course
of history or, in other words, a theory of universal history. The
concept of universal history is Pannenberg's chief contribution to the debates on hermeneutics (1963). It is also the context of his argument for theology as 'scientific' knowledge.
When he argues that the history of religions and the history of
Christianity should become the theology of religion and the
theology of Christianity and thus the science of God, offering a
body of knowledge on God, he is reasserting his contention
that God's self-revelation is not direct in the manner of a
theophany, but indirect through history and that revelation as
history is accessible to historical investigation.

A different attempt to give an account of theology in the context of recent theoretical discussions about scientific, that is,
methodically organized, knowledge is to be found in Helmut
Peukert's *Wissenschaftstheorie – Handlungstheorie – fundamentale
Theologie* (1976). Peukert enters more closely into the present
problematic of the philosophy of science in regard to both the

natural and the social sciences. His contention is that the questions at present raised in the theory of science converge upon the question of communicative action, namely action among subjects aimed at achieving a mutual understanding.

Again and again, discussions about the nature of scientific inquiry and scientific theory have, he says, brought philosophers of science up against the question of communication within the scientific community, the nodal point of a variety of problems, such as the limits of any formal system, ordinary language as the basis and context for formal scientific discourse, the logic of scientific revolutions, the recognition that the empirical sciences could no longer ignore their own history nor in that way escape the hermeneutic problematic. Such problems have created a new interest in linguistics, particularly in pragmatics, the systematic study of the structure and conditions of speech situations. On the other hand, the intersubjective, as distinct from the objective, level of communication has long been central to the problematic of the social sciences when not behaviouristically conceived, and in them, too, there is an increasing concern with speech acts and with pragmatics. A theory of communicative action would seem, then, to provide a common basis on which to ground a comprehensive theory of scientific knowledge.

Having ascertained that, Peukert goes on to develop his theological thesis, which is that a theory of communicative action also provides a fundamental theology, namely a basic theory on which to ground theology as a science. Communicative action has dimensions and raises problems that can be handled only theologically. To mention themes such as universal solidarity in freedom or the unconditional acceptance of the other may give some indication of what he has in mind. A theory of communicative action, therefore, opens out into a fundamental theology, which will offer a theological theory of communicative action, of the subject, of society and of history. Thus, the point where theology and *Wissenschaftstheorie* or the theory of scientific knowledge meet is the theory of communicative action, which grounds the rationality both of the sciences and of theology.

My present interest in Peukert's thesis comes from its connection with Habermas's theory of communicative competence, upon which Peukert draws. Habermas's theory is important for political theology, because in his analysis of communicative competence he claims to have uncovered the normative foundation of every linguistic communication and thus of society. Underlying every speech situation, according to his analysis, is an orientation towards truth, freedom and justice, and, consequently, an anticipation of an emancipated form of life, in which autonomy and responsibility are possible. In that fashion the normative foundation presupposed in speech becomes the point of departure for the critical theory of society (1971b: 141). Albrecht Wellmer has spoken of a 'linguistic turn in critical theory' (O'Neill, ed., 1976: 231ff). In other words, the long effort of the critical theory of society, associated with the Frankfurt School, to find a rational foundation for the critique of ideology and for the emancipatory struggle has eventually led in Habermas to an identification of that foundation with norms discerned as inherent in all speech. These norms implicit in every instance of speech are capable of articulation in a universal pragmatics, that is, in a systematic investigation of the general structures of every possible speech situation.

Dietrich Böhler has pointed out (1970b: 223) that behind the work of Habermas lies the same problem that troubled Max Horkheimer, the founder of the critical theory, namely, how to avoid making the emancipatory interest purely arbitrary, which it would be if it were seen as being simply the existential decision of individuals, which as such is outside the sphere of rational discussion. There is need of an orientation that points beyond every actual situation or, as Böhler describes it, of a demythologized, eschatological dynamic. To put the problem in another way: it is a question of 'substantial or objective reason' versus 'instrumental or formal reason'. Horkheimer with some pathos describes the outcome of the exclusive dominance of a rationality conceived as a purely formal, technical instrument:

What are the consequences of the formalization of reason? Justice, equality, happiness, tolerance, all the concepts that, as mentioned, were in preceding centuries supposed to be inherent in or sanctioned by reason, have lost their intellectual roots. They are still aims and ends, but there is no rational agency authorized to appraise and link them to an objective reality. Endorsed by venerable historical documents, they may still enjoy a certain prestige, and some are contained in the supreme law of the greatest countries. Nevertheless, they lack any confirmation by reason in its modern sense. Who can say that any one of these ideals is more closely related to truth than its opposite? According to the philosophy of the average modern intellectual, there is only one authority, namely, science, conceived as the classification of facts and the calculation of probabilities. The statement that justice and freedom are better in themselves than injustice and oppression is scientifically unverifiable and useless. It has come to sound as meaningless in itself as would the statement that red is more beautiful than blue, or that an egg is better than milk (1974: 23–4).

Is there a different kind of rationality, a rationality that can philosophically ground the emancipatory option, together with its critical analysis of the present historical situation, in order to change it?

That is the problem which has exercised the mind of Habermas. In response to it he has invoked a theory of communicative competence as providing a starting-point for a comprehensive theory of rationality, embracing both theoretical and practical reason and serving as the rational foundation for the emancipatory interest. 'The human interest', he writes, 'in autonomy and responsibility is not mere fancy, for it can be apprehended a priori. What raises us out of nature is the only thing whose nature we can know: *language*. Through its structure, autonomy and responsibility are posited for us. Our first sentence expresses unequivocally the intention of universal and unconstrained consensus' (1972b: 314 – Habermas's italics).

What Habermas claims to have done is to have found a self-sufficient rational argument for the emancipatory values. The question I want to raise in this chapter is, Has he succeeded? In other words, Has he provided for freedom an argument which stands independent of tradition, so that in working for emancipation we need no longer appeal to the great moral and religious traditions, but can replace their authority with autonomous reason? To answer the question we must first make sure we understand the claim of Habermas by placing it in the context of his work as a whole.

We can approach the writings of Habermas by observing

that he shares the opposition of his elders in the Frankfurt School, Horkheimer and Adorno, to positivism. Positivism may be roughly defined as the equation of technical or instrumental rationality with rationality as a whole, together with a refusal of reflection (Adorno *et al.*, 1976). The book of Habermas, *Knowledge and Human Interests*, is a pre-history of modern positivism, tracing the replacement of theories of knowledge, representing transcendental reflection, by the philosophy of science, interpreted positivistically, which means by scientism. Scientism refuses transcendental reflection upon the conditions of possible knowledge. Its principle, as formulated by Habermas, is 'that the meaning of knowledge is defined by what the sciences do and can thus be adequately explicated through the methodological analysis of scientific procedures. Any epistemology that transcends the framework of methodology as such now succumbs to the same sentence of extravagance and meaninglessness that it once passed on metaphysics' (1972b: 67). Nevertheless, despite its theoretical exclusion, reflection upon the processes of research in the natural and human sciences did in fact continue, and this eventually brought about new approaches to science and again raised the transcendental question. Further, as Habermas sees it, psychoanalysis represents a unique development. Despite the mistaken, scientistic self-understanding of Freud, psychoanalysis is the first instance of a science that methodically uses self-reflection. In short, according to Habermas, the time is now ripe for a revival of transcendental philosophy. He himself describes his work as setting forth 'the conception of a new and transformed transcendental philosophy' (1973b: 165). His systematic analysis of the relation between knowledge and human interests, outlined in the last chapter, is intended as a first attempt in that direction.

Habermas, it will be recalled, refuses to postulate a transcendental subject distinct from empirical, naturally generated and socially formed subjects. The three interests, which, as deep-seated invariants, constitute the three modes of knowledge, are therefore said to have a quasi-transcendental status, the qualification indicating that, though they have a transcendental function as *a priori* invariants, they have an empirical basis in the history of society, from which they are derived and in which they remain grounded.

The three interests, then, are rooted in the various dynamic or formative elements through which society comes into existence: the technical interest has its roots in work, the practical in ordinary language communication and the emancipatory in power as a means of social organization.

Work and ordinary language communication require further consideration, because they are the two basic kinds of human action. Since society is the co-ordination of human action, the understanding of society demands that we distinguish the different kinds of human action and the manner of their co-ordination.

Work, as Habermas understands it, is what Weber called purposive–rational (*zweckrational*) action. This is action directed to success in achieving some concrete end by organized means. It is found in two different forms. When the action is aimed at a successful physical intervention through some technical means it is called instrumental action. Instrumental action is thus governed by technical rules based on empirical knowledge. Purposive–rational action may also take the form of strategic action. Strategic action is the kind of action studied in decision theory and game theory. It follows rules of rational choice based on analytic knowledge, namely on deductions drawn from value systems and decision procedures. Instrumental action is evaluated according to its efficacy in intervening in the physical state of affairs. We evaluate strategic action by its success in influencing the decisions of others through the calculative schemes it puts into effect. These two types of action together form the context of life and experience from which arises the knowledge which is then systematized and developed in the empirical–analytic sciences.

In contrast to purposive–rational action, there is communicative action, occurring in the social medium of ordinary language. Communicative action is directed towards reaching an understanding among people, who are not therefore seeking their own success, but trying to come to an agreement. With an agreement achieved communicatively we are on a different level of social interaction than with systems of purposive–rational action.

How are human actions co-ordinated? Purposive–rational

actions can be co-ordinated merely instrumentally or strategi-cally into systems. Instrumental co-ordination is by empiri-cally effective means, that is, by violence. Strategic co-ordination is by competition or manipulation. When other people are treated purely instrumentally as though they were physical objects to be used in achieving success in one's pro-posed end, then there is a co-ordination of human action through violence. With strategic co-ordination one does not treat other persons simply as physical objects, but takes account of their decisions, intentions and plans. But one does so in order to influence their decisions either by overtly calcu-lative schemes or covertly with deception by manipulation. Success in achieving one's own end is still the aim, but the actions of oneself and of others are co-ordinated, not by vio-lence, but strategically.

Both forms of human action, the instrumental and strategic, and both forms of co-ordination, by violence and by strategy, fall short of creating human society. Human society demands communicative action, where people are not aiming at success in achieving their own individual purpose, but at an agree-ment achieved by interaction. If one looks at bourgeois society from that standpoint, then one can see how it fell short of being a truly human society. The relation between the capita-lists and the workers was instrumental. The capitalists used the workers simply as hands or physical factors in the process of production; the workers were brought by compulsion or violence to co-ordinate their action with that of the capitalists. At the same time, the relation of the capitalists among them-selves was competitive, namely strategic. What was pushed into the background was the level of communicative action, on which alone a human society can be built.

Communicative action is governed by consensual norms, held in a communicatively achieved agreement or at least intersubjectively presupposed. The context of communicative action is the life-world, understood as the total network of nor-matively regulated interpersonal relations. Within that social context arises knowledge in the form of interpretations, which is then elaborated into the systematic understanding of mean-ing and traditions set forth in the hermeneutic and historical disciplines.

Habermas has not only rejected positivism and scientism, but has also shown himself acutely aware of their harmful repercussions upon society, as instanced in the emergence of a technocratic society. He even sees a neglect of the distinctive character of communicative action as producing a scientistic distortion within Marx's own thought, resulting in the later false objectivism of dialectical materialism. There is therefore no doubt that he is strongly opposed to the claim of the empirical–analytic sciences to a monopoly of knowledge.

Nonetheless, as Dieter Misgeld remarks, it 'amounts to a major reorientation of critical theory, then, when Juergen Habermas adopts hermeneutical reflection as a viable orientation in the logic of social science, and enlists its support for a critique of the objectivist features of empirical–analytic social . . .' (O'Neill, ed., 1976: 165). Hermeneutics and critique of ideology are usually considered as opposing approaches, hermeneutics being based on a positive evaluation of tradition, critique of ideology on a negative assessment.

The difference may be seen in the contrasting attitudes to the Enlightenment.

Gadamer, the leading proponent of hermeneutic philosophy, criticizes the Enlightenment for setting up an opposition between reason on the one hand and authority and tradition on the other. He speaks of 'the rehabilitation of authority and tradition' (1975: 245). Adorno and Horkheimer of the Frankfurt School also criticize the Enlightenment, but for its falling into the myth of total control of nature, with the consequence that has had of an attempted control over men, not for its stress upon the autonomy of reason over against authority. Critical theology aims at an emancipatory critique of traditions as originating in structures of social domination and being thus places of distorted communication and untruths. In brief, it has taken up the Enlightenment critique of authority and tradition.

Habermas, however, sees hermeneutics as complementing the empirical–analytic sciences in the comprehensive account he gives of the modes of knowledge. All the same, just as he refuses the exclusive claims of positivism, so also he rejects the claim of universality made by Gadamer's hermeneutic philosophy. Further, he continues to insist upon the need for critique in regard to tradition in a manner which in effect dissolves the authority of tradition. He distinguishes the interpretation and application of tradition in hermeneutics from a critical appropriation of tradition. Critical appropriation releases the content of meaning in tradition, while refusing any claim that cannot be reduced in rational discourse (1976a: 70). In a similar fashion, he regards a normative agreement based on tradition as lower on the scale of rationality than one reached through rationally grounded procedures of will-formation (1977: 202). Therefore, Habermas's recognition of the distinctive place of the hermeneutic and historical disciplines is by no means an acceptance of the authority of tradition.

However, before we pursue the question of tradition versus self-sufficient reason, some words are necessary on the third cognitive interest, the emancipatory, on Habermas's conception of critique as a mode of knowledge and on the distinction he has introduced between action and discourse.

Richard Bernstein rightly observes that 'important and difficult problems concern Habermas' systematic attempt to articulate and justify critique as a distinctive form of knowledge with its own epistemological integrity' (1976: 205). I should add that, apart from the intrinsic difficulties, there is the fact that Habermas's thought is always on the move, and it is no easy task to follow it through its successive developments.

He states that the emancipatory interest is derivative in status:

Compared with the technical and practical interests in knowledge, which are both grounded in deeply rooted (invariant?) structures of action and experience – i.e. in the constituent elements of social systems – the *emancipatory interest in knowledge* has a derivative status. It guarantees the connection between theoretical knowledge and an 'object domain' of practical life which comes into existence as a result of systematically distorted communication and thinly legitimated repression. The type of action and experience corresponding to this object domain is, therefore, also derivative (1973a: 176 – Habermas's italics).

I find that statement confusing. It is true that 'the structure of distorted communication is not ultimate' (1974a: 17), so that, in that sense, 'this interest can only develop to the degree to which repressive force, in the form of the normative exercise of power, presents itself permanently in structures of distorted communication – that is, to the extent that domination is institutionalized' (*ibid.*, 22). All the same, the structure of distorted communication has, Habermas says, 'its basis in the logic of undistorted language communication' (*ibid.*, 17). Now, as we shall see, he argues in his universal pragmatics that all speech implies the anticipation of an ideal speech situation, which means a situation free from all external and internal constraints. His analysis of this ideal speech situation uncovers as inherent in it truth, freedom and justice or, in other words, an emancipated form of life. Thus anticipated in every act of communication is a situation defined precisely by that freedom from constraint which is the content of the emancipatory interest. But to argue in that way makes the emancipatory interest both basic and comprehensive. It grounds speech concerning technical and practical questions as well as the properly emancipatory or therapeutic discourse directed to the dissolution of unrecognized, repressive constraints. For that reason, Bernstein speaks of the emancipatory interest as 'at once derivative, and the most basic cognitive interest' (1976: 198). But that is to state rather than to clarify the confusion. Here I can simply note that there is a basic *a priori* normative interest in freedom, which in the concrete circumstances of repression becomes an emancipatory interest.[12]

To understand Habermas's conception of critique as a mode of knowledge, we need to introduce the distinction he makes in his more recent writings between reconstruction and self-reflection.

The term 'reflection', drawn from German idealism, he now finds covers two things. There is, first, the type of reflection found in Kant in the form of a search for the transcendental ground or subjective conditions of possibility of knowledge. More recently, this type of reflection has dropped the transcendental subject and become the rational reconstruction of generative rules and cognitive schemata, as for example in general linguistics. The second type of reflection comes from Hegel's idea of the critical dissolution of subjectively constituted pseudo-objectivity, that is, of an analytical emancipation from objective illusions. Freud took this notion of self-criticism out of its epistemological context and applied it to an empirical subject as overcoming illusions about its own being. That second type of reflection coincides with critique (Habermas, 1973a: 182–3).[13]

What Habermas has in mind becomes clearer when he distinguishes the reconstructive sciences, the genetic sciences and the critical sciences.

The reconstructive sciences are those like logic, general linguistics, universal pragmatics, which organize a knowledge arising out of pure reconstructive reflection. They provide a transformed epistemology, reconstructing generative rules without postulating a transcendental subject. At this point Habermas inserts a contention, important for his attempt to find a self-sufficient rational basis for emancipatory values. He maintains that moral philosophy can achieve the status of a reconstructive science as a communicative or linguistic ethic (*Sprachethik*), that is, by deriving universal ethical rules from the fundamental norms presupposed in every instance of rational speech (1973a: 183; 1976a: 102–10). Reconstructive knowledge falls outside Habermas's earlier scheme of three cognitive interests. It does not come under either the technical or the practical interest. Its relation to the emancipatory interest is only indirect, that is, in so far as reconstructive knowledge is taken up into critical self-reflection. What directly gives rise to reconstructive knowledge is said to be a 'reflexive attitude', an impulse within discourse, leading us to reflect upon the conditions we unreflectively rely upon whenever we engage in rational speech (1974a: 24).

Besides the horizontal type of reconstruction found in the pure reconstructive sciences, there is a vertical type of reconstruction, which has led to the genetic sciences. 'These sciences', writes Habermas, 'are at once reconstructive and empirical in their approach in that they try to explain the development or acquisition of cognitive, linguistic, and communicative competences in terms of reconstructable logical patterns *and* empirical mechanisms' (1973a: 184 – Habermas's italics). Genetic reconstruction may be ontogenetic and applied to explain the acquisition of speech and of moral consciousness. Habermas cites the work of Chomsky and Piaget. It may also be phylogenetic and used in explaining the development of productive forces and those epochal changes of institutional structures which are connected with changes of world-view and the evolution of moral systems. Here may be placed the work of Marx to the extent that historical materialism is a theoretical explanation of social evolution (Habermas and Luhmann, 1971: 171–5, n. 2).

Theories from both the reconstructive and the genetic sciences are constitutive of the critical sciences. The critical sciences are psychoanalysis and critique of ideology, the latter being the critical as distinct from the nomological function of the social sciences. The critical sciences make self-reflection into a scientific method. Self-reflection itself is a hermeneutic or interpretative procedure, but one of a peculiar kind. In it 'the method of *Verstehen*' is linked 'with the objectivating procedures of causal–analytical science' (Adorno *et al.*, 1976: 140). In other words, it uses causal theories from the reconstructive and genetic sciences to produce interpretations of neurotically and ideologically distorted communication. It is because self-reflection thus draws upon explanatory theories of the causal–analytic type that it results in an explanatory understanding, in which the usual hermeneutic understanding is widened to critique (Habermas, 1970b: 158).

The critical *interpretations* produced in the process of self-reflection are validated, according to Habermas, by the acceptance of those concerned. They confirm the interpretations by recognizing themselves in them. The *theories* used in producing the explanatory interpretations are subject to scientific discourse. Nevertheless, the acceptance of those involved constitutes a second level of validation for the theories themselves.[14]

The question of the validation of theories confronts us with a distinction Habermas has introduced in his later writings and which now plays an important part in his thought: the distinction between action and discourse.

By action he means the realm of living, where people act and experience. In the sphere of living the claims to validity made in speech are so embedded in contexts of action that they can be only naively accepted or rejected. When the claims become problematical, there is a transition to discourse. Discourse is that form of communication which is disengaged from action and experience in which we enter into argument. The claims are treated as hypothetical and through argument are rationally grounded or rejected. Such discursive testing of hypothetical claims to validity requires a suspension or virtualization of the pressures of action and experience. 'In a discourse', Habermas writes, 'the "force" of the argument is the only permissible compulsion, whereas the co-operative search for truth is the only permissible motive. Because of their communicative structure, discourses do not compel their participants to act. Nor do they accommodate processes whereby information can be *acquired*. They are purged of action and experience' (1973a: 168 – Habermas's italics).

Habermas goes on to state that 'the *a priori* of experience (which lays down the structure of the objects of possible experience) is independent of the *a priori* of argumentative reasoning (which lays down the conditions of possible discourse)' (*ibid.*, 171).

This renders the function of the cognitive interests more precise. They operate directly only in the realm of action. The technical and practical interests become the transcendental framework within which we organize our experience prior to science. These interests make possible the objectivation of reality, that is, the constitution of two different object domains. The technical interest establishes the object domain of things and events, the practical interest that of persons and utterances. Habermas describes the constitution of the twofold object domain in this way:

In the functional sphere of instrumental action we encounter objects of the type of moving bodies; here we experience things, events, and conditions which are, in principle, capable of being manipulated. In interactions (or at the level of possible intersubjective communication) we encounter objects of the type of speaking and acting subjects; here we experience persons, utterances and conditions which in principle are structured and to be understood symbolically. The object domains of the empirical–analytic and of the hermeneutic sciences are based on these objectifications of reality, which we undertake daily always from the viewpoint either of technical control or intersubjective communication (1974a: 8).

The object domains of the various sciences merely continue the objectivations we make, prior to all science, in the realm of life and experience, where the two cognitive interests are directly operative. Hence the cognitive interests in objectivating our experience are thereby constituting the objects about which theoretical statements are possible in the sciences. They thus form a link between action and discourse.

The emancipatory interest again stands apart from the other two. As far as its object domain is concerned, the emancipatory interest in the narrow sense is derivative, because it relates to the emergence of structures of repression. Further, the self-reflection to which it directly gives rise has a peculiar relation to discourse. The process of self-reflection is not properly a discourse, because those involved, for example the doctor and patient in a psychoanalytic dialogue, are not equal partners. On the other hand, therapeutic discourse, remaining as it does bound to action and experience, achieves more than an ordinary discourse. It results in an insight that satisfies, not only the claim to truth (or correctness), but also the claim to authenticity or truthfulness, the absence of deception, both of oneself and of others; and this is not something that can be attained by ordinary discourse.

Perhaps at the expense of some repetition I should try now to give a general summary of Habermas's account of knowledge.

He distinguishes three areas: action or the realm of living or *praxis (Lebenspraxis)*, discourse and reflection.

Within action or the sphere of experience and living are two basic interests, through which reality is objectivated. The technical interest, linked to the social medium of work, establishes the object domain of things and events and is the *a priori* condition of technical knowledge and action. The practical interest, linked to the social medium or ordinary language communication, establishes the object domain of persons and utterances and is the *a priori* condition of interpretative knowledge and communicative action. It should be noted, however, that technical knowledge and the purposive–rational action it guides only occur and are shared among persons within the context of social interaction. Hence the entire area of action or living, at least ideally when undistorted, may as a whole including technical knowledge and activity be taken as communicative action in relation to discourse, which redeems all its validity claims.

Within the area of action, domination arises as a social medium. From this comes the pseudo-object domain of structures of distorted communication, which evokes the emancipatory interest. Directly governed by this emancipatory interest emerges the process of self-reflection, which, unlike discourse, remains within the area of action and living.

Over against action is discourse, which requires a suspension of the demands of action. Discourse takes up the assertive and normative claims implicit in communicative action. The assertive claims are argumentatively established in theoretical discourse, the normative claims in practical discourse. Theoretical discourse is differentiated according to the two object domains constituted in the realm of action. Hence at the level of discourse there are the empirical–analytic sciences and the hermeneutic–historical disciplines.

Reflection in the sense of reconstruction is a distinctive line of discourse. It gives rise to the pure reconstructive sciences, such as logic and universal pragmatics, and then, in combination with the empirical–analytic and hermeneutic–historical sciences, to the genetic sciences. Both these types of reconstructive theory enter into the process of self-reflection or emancipatory critique, but self-reflection itself is not properly speaking discourse. Critique, then, for Habermas has two levels: the level of critical theory, which is a reconstructive type of knowledge, demanding justification in theoretical discourse, and the process of enlightenment or self-reflection, in which the critical theories are brought to bear upon the concrete situation of an individual or group.

That impressive analysis with its formidable array of distinctions raises many questions. Our direct interest here, however, is where in Habermas's account he finds a self-sufficient rational ground for the emancipatory values that constitute the normative element in critique. A rather lengthy exposition of his general synthesis seemed a necessary preliminary, because Habermas is a major thinker, too original to be approached casually, whose thought is not yet widely familiar, at least in theological circles. His writings represent the most powerful recent attempt to ground human freedom and an emancipated society upon autonomous reason. He himself finds Marx's theory of society, to which in general he adheres, unclear and defective in regard to its normative basis. In seeking to remedy that defect, Habermas has turned to a theory of communication as a resource for reconstructing historical materialism (1976b: 10–12). Hence in his recent writings he has concentrated upon universal pragmatics, namely upon a theory of communication. It is through the analysis of the *a priori* conditions of discourse as worked out in his theory of communication that he finds the normative basis for the emancipatory values.

Universal pragmatics is the rational reconstruction of the general structures that are found in every possible speech situation. It is distinct from empirical pragmatics, which, as in psycho- and socio-linguistics, studies the extra-linguistic, empirical and contingent limiting conditions of actual communication. Universal pragmatics exhibits the ability of the adult speaker to structure modes of communication or set up the speech situation. This is what Habermas calls a communicative competence from analogy with Chomsky's linguistic competence. Although the pragmatic features of a speech situation need not be expressly verbalized, they can be made explicit with the aid of linguistic elements, called the dialogue-constitutive or pragmatic universals: for example, the performative verbs, such as 'assert', 'promise', 'command', which determine the sense of the utterance, the relation of the speaker to it and the relation of speaker to hearer.

The elementary unit of speech is the speech act. Every speech act has a double structure. It produces and represents a particular mode of interpersonal relationship between a speaker and a hearer. This is the illocutionary component. Within that relationship some content is communicated. This is the propositional component. In a constative speech act, in which the content is asserted, the propositional component assumes the form of a proposition. In non-constative speech acts, such as a promise or command, the propositional content is not asserted, but only mentioned.

There are, then, two levels of communication: the level of intersubjectivity, on which the speaker and hearer, through illocutionary acts, bring about the interpersonal relationship that allows them to achieve mutual understanding; and the level of objects in the world or states of affairs about which they want to achieve a consensus within the terms of that relationship. A speech act can succeed only if speaker and hearer communicate on both levels at once and thus fulfil the double structure of speech (1976c: 157).

Every speech act carries with it four different types of validity claims. There is, first, the claim to the truth of its propositional component. This claim is clearly focussed in constative speech acts, in which a proposition is asserted, but, though less clearly demarcated, it is attached to the propositional content of non-constative speech acts. Second, there is the truthfulness the speaker claims for the expression of his intention. This validity claim receives special emphasis in expressive speech acts, in which a speaker articulates a feeling, makes a confession, reveals something and so on, but in other speech acts, such as assertions or promises, the claim to truthfulness is implied. The third claim is the claim the speaker makes to the rightness of his action in relation to a given normative context (or mediately for this context itself). This type of claim becomes most clear in institutionally regulated speech acts, such as baptizing, marrying, betting and so on, which directly fulfil determinate norms. But all speech acts through their illocutionary component give rise to interpersonal relations, and these cannot arise except in a normative context. Hence the normative validity claim is universally built into the structure of speech. Finally, there is the claim for the comprehensibility of the utterance.

In communicative action or, in other words, in the realm of living and experience, these claims are accepted naively. They are taken for granted as elements of an underlying consensus on which functioning language games are based. They can, however, be challenged. The claim to comprehensibility must be worked out in fact through whatever further interaction is needed. Likewise, the claim to truthfulness can be tested only through interaction. Time will show whether the other party is acting truthfully or is engaged in deception. The other two claims, namely to truth and to rightness, if fundamentally contested in a way that cannot be met by further information or clarification, can be redeemed only by discourse. Theoretical discourse deals with the truth of a problematical assertion, practical discourse with the rightness or correctness of a problematical norm. Communicative action, therefore, in general contains an implicit reference to discourse; it implies the possibility of discourse, should the existing consensus come under question.

Habermas then argues that discourse itself implies the counterfactual supposition of the ideal speech situation. In other words, the ideal speech situation is presupposed and anticipated by discourse. It is a potentiality inherent in the present situation, though never completely realized.

Why does discourse presuppose the ideal speech situation? It does so because to take part in a discourse is to suppose that a genuine agreement is possible. Discourse would be rendered a meaningless procedure if a grounded consensus were not possible or could not be distinguished from a false consensus. Discursive justification is thus a normative concept. Habermas holds a consensus theory of truth (1973b), but for him the truth of an opinion or the rightness of a norm is not merely the fact that a consensus has been realized, but that it is a rationally grounded consensus. When is a consensus rationally grounded? Habermas maintains that a rational consensus can be characterized only formally. It is one achieved in unrestrained and universal discourse, that is, a discourse free from all constraint, whether accidental or systematic, where the only force is the force of the better argument and where there is an equal distribution of chances to participate. In other words, a consensus is rationally grounded only in so far as the discourse presupposes and anticipates the ideal speech situation. 'Ideal speech', writes Bernstein in his account of Habermas, 'is that form of discourse in which there is no other compulsion but the compulsion of argumentation itself; where there is a genuine symmetry among the participants involved, allowing a universal interchangeability of dialogue roles; where no form of domination exists. The power of ideal speech is the power of argumentation itself' (1976: 212).

If we now follow up the requirements of the ideal speech situation, we find that they imply an ideal form of social life, a form where the organization of society in its institutions and practices allows free, symmetrical and unconstrained discourse. The requirements of symmetry, while calling for a word of explanation, are particularly weighted with consequences. Clearly, in regard to the discourse itself, everyone should have an equal opportunity to open or continue the discussion and also be equally able to join in by putting forward statements and arguments and countering those of others, with no one's opinion exempted from consideration or criticism. But the principle of symmetry also implies conditions relating directly, not to the discourse itself, but to the organization of the realm of action or living, and yet being indirectly necessary to ensure a discourse free from constraint. Those taking part in the discourse must be so situated that they are able to express themselves, their attitudes, their feelings, their intentions openly without constraint, because only thus will their participation be truthful and sincere. Further, everyone taking part must be equally placed in regard to such regulative speech acts, such as commanding, permitting, forbidding, and so on. In other words, there must be no privileges in the sense of any unequally binding norms. Consequently, ideal speech implies a society free from domination, organized on a principle of equality and embodying the ideals of truth, freedom and justice.

What, then, is the status of the ideal speech situation? In Habermas's words, it is 'neither an empirical phenomenon nor simply a construct, but a reciprocal supposition or imputation (*Unterstellung*) unavoidable in discourse. This supposition can, but need not be, contra-factual; but even when contra-factual it is a fiction which is operatively effective in communication' (1973b: 258; translation from McCarthy, 1976: 486). He therefore prefers, the passage continues, to speak of an anticipation of an ideal speech situation, an anticipation that alone allows us to qualify any actually attained consensus as rational and at the same time serves as a critical standard against which any actual consensus can be questioned and tested.

The sequence of Habermas's whole argument for a communication theory of society has been neatly summarized by McCarthy in this passage:

The analysis of speech shows it to be oriented toward the idea of truth. The analysis of 'truth' leads to the notion of a discursively achieved consensus. The analysis of 'consensus' shows this concept to involve a normative dimension. The analysis of the notion of a grounded consensus ties it to a speech situation which is free from all external and internal constraints, that is, in which the resulting consensus is due simply to the force of the better argument. Finally, the analysis of the ideal speech situation shows it to involve assumptions about the context of interaction in which speech is located. The end result of this chain of argument is that the very structure of speech involves the anticipation of a form of life in which autonomy and responsibility are possible. 'The critical theory of society takes this as its point of departure.' Its normative foundation is therefore not arbitrary, but inherent in the very structure of social action which it analyses (*ibid.*, 495).

Such, then, is Habermas's argument for the rational, normative basis of an emancipated society. Does he succeed in showing how we may rationally ground freedom? I use the word 'freedom' as a convenient designation for the entire complex of values we have in mind when we speak of emancipation or human liberation.

Habermas, to sum up, gives a twofold answer to the question of the rational grounding of freedom. First, concerning the method of grounding: when freedom becomes problematical as a value, its claim to validity, like that of norms and values in general, can be redeemed only by argumentation or discourse. Second, concerning the grounds themselves: because to take part in discourse is implicitly to acknowledge freedom as a value, discourse presupposes and anticipates freedom, so that discourse itself when analysed provides the transcendental grounds that make a discursively reached agreement on freedom a rational consensus.

For me that twofold thesis is an exaggeration of the function and meaning of theoretical reason. Argumentation of its nature, I contend, can be neither the chief means nor the chief grounds of a rational consensus on freedom. Because of its complexity and ambiguity, freedom more than other moral values must first be an experience before it can become a principle, and no one can talk about it intelligently or wisely as a principle without having experienced it as a reality. Freedom is a social and cumulative experience; it is preserved and transmitted only as an historical form of life, namely a tradition. The entry to that tradition is by shared action, not by discourse.

Tradition is the ground of values, not as an external or heteronomous authority, but as their real presence in history. Tradition cannot be bypassed, because human historical experience is not linear. There are qualitatively different moments where a unique convergence of events or the advent of a uniquely endowed person causes an originative experience, to the heights of which subsequent generations must strive by memory. Memory thus brings together reason and history. Such memory is not a dogmatic imposition, but an encounter with the reality of an historically embodied value.

Habermas himself admits that ideal discourse requires an ideal social situation. The extent to which the ideal social situation is absent is the extent to which any discourse will be lacking in rationality. It would seem to follow that if the social situation renders freedom seriously problematical, discourse will be impotent to meet the difficulty. How can freedom be grounded by a discourse free from constraint when such discourse is possible only if freedom has been attained?

As a manifestation of rationality discourse or argumentation is severely limited in its efficacy and meaning. Even supposing a discourse unconstrained by domination, what reason is there to suppose that continued argumentation will resolve conflicts of opinion or norms? Such conflicts may often be more effectively resolved on the level of experience and action. Common participation in the Resistance did more to achieve mutual understanding between Christians and Marxists in France than years of argumentation would have achieved. From the opposite standpoint, Alvin Gouldner has pertinently questioned whether violence 'is always and necessarily inimical to *rationality*'. Referring to the use of torture, he says: 'Under some conditions, then, it seems violence is expected to (and perhaps *does*) *remove*, rather than impose, communication distortions. Indeed under some conditions violent actions themselves constitute *ambiguity-reducing communications* unmistakenly saying where those who engage in them stand, and what they are willing to do to achieve their ends' (1976: 142–3 – Gouldner's italics). One may with Gouldner detest violence and yet recognize that sometimes it has the effect of bringing an increase of rationality into a situation by counteracting or removing other, more disturbing, irrational factors.

Again, how far does the other requirement for discourse, namely a symmetry in the chances to participate, promote rationality? McCarthy remarks:

At the level of theoretic explanation – for example, in the natural sciences or in mathematics – what counts as rational discourse does not seem to require this symmetry, does not seem to be incompatible with any number of psychological, moral or political, peculiarities of the participants so long as these do not occasion a departure from the standards accepted within their discipline (1976: 391).

But further, the equality within discourse postulated by Habermas is feasible only in a limited environment and does not correspond to the general conditions of human history. Certainly, a discourse may be distorted by domination, that is, by the failure of one participant, endowed with power, to allow other participants their say. Nevertheless, people differ widely in their reflective capacities and, more importantly, in their moral worth. The exclusion of domination does not mean an equality of endowment or an absence of cultural disparity. The acknowledgement of superiority in the master–disciple relationship that binds religious leaders and their followers need not be irrational. After all, it is questionable whether the kind of discussion among equals found in a university seminar is appropriate as a model for the wider human community. Habermas's ideal speech situation can too easily become the postulate of a non-historical place from which to consider and assess the distortions of actual human communication.

The attitude of Habermas to tradition is given detailed expression in his controversy with Gadamer.[15] Running through Gadamer's *Truth and Method* is a contrast between the alienation (*Verfremdung*), brought about by the distancing from its objects in modern scientific method, and the be-longingness (*Zugehörigkeit*), which hermeneutical reflection uncovers as the primary and ineluctable relationship. In the three parts of *Truth and Method*, Gadamer unfolds this contrast with reference to art, history and language respectively. He argues that belongingness comes first in each sphere, preceding and making possible the objectifying experience as required by modern scientific method. On the basis of the opposition between belongingness and alienation, Gadamer rehabilitates prejudice or pre-judgement (*Vorurteil*), authority and tradition. Human beings are finite, and this finitude implies that they find themselves within a tradition or traditions. We are all immersed in a history that precedes both us and our reflection upon it. Hence prejudice precedes judgement and acceptance of traditions precedes any examination of those traditions.

Against this, Habermas argues that the reflective appropriation of tradition has the effect of breaking the unplanned course of its spontaneous growth (*naturwüchsige Substanz*) and of altering the relationship of persons to it. Gadamer, he insists, misunderstands the power of reflection as released and made effective in understanding (*Verstehen*). Understanding destroys the apparent absoluteness of a tradition and makes clear its contingent character. The dogmatism of a traditional mode of life is destroyed. In other words, although its content is appropriated, tradition ceases to operate as tradition. In a similar way, understanding affects prejudices. When a structure of pre-judgements has been made transparent by reflection, it can no longer function as a set of prejudices.

Gadamer retorts by rejecting the opposition Habermas sets up between the unplanned course of tradition (*naturwüchsige Tradition*) and the reflective appropriation of tradition. No doubt, reflection brings something before my mind which otherwise takes place, as it were, behind my back, but tradition cannot totally be thus confronted and objectified. He refers to his concept of effective historical consciousness (*wirkungsgeschichtliches Bewusstsein*), which means a consciousness of being so immersed in history that it is impossible to stand over against it in a free, independent, objectifying way. This implies that our reflection is conditioned and finite, and therefore is not such as to take away the power of tradition.

One may well agree with Ricoeur (1973: 52), who in general is closer to Gadamer than to Habermas, that Gadamer does not do justice to the critical moment of reflection and the detachment it requires. Nevertheless, without going all the way with Gadamer, it is still possible to question Habermas's contention that hermeneutical understanding in effect halts the working of tradition. In *Legitimation Crisis* Habermas distinguishes between hermeneutics, which destroys the nature-like working of tradition while keeping its authority at the reflective level, and critique, which appropriates the content of tradition, but replaces the claims it makes as tradition with discursive reason (1976a: 70). But does he take sufficient account of the hermeneutic element that persists in all our knowledge?

Habermas ties hermeneutic procedures to ordinary language communication. He then goes on to assert that modern science formulates true propositions, not reached through ordinary language with its dialogic structure, but through various monological procedures. Hypothetical–deductive sets of propositions do not belong to talk. The information derived from them stands at a distance from the life-world as articulated in ordinary language. He admits that the results of technically utilizable knowledge have to be brought into ordinary language. The monologically acquired scientific knowledge has to be translated into the dialogic language of everyday life. But fundamentally scientific knowledge lies outside ordinary language. He refers to Piaget's genetic account of knowledge as showing the roots of operative thought to be independent of language. Categories such as space, time, causality and substance and the rules for formal symbolic structures have a pre-linguistic basis. Hence the monological use of language for the organization of purposive–rational action and for scientific theories does not come within the intersubjective structure of ordinary language communication. This, Habermas contends, places a limit upon hermeneutics. The conditions of understanding of scientific discourse are not those of ordinary language communication. For that reason scientific discourse does not come under the hermeneutical approach. It does so only when the content of scientific theory is brought into relationship with the life-world (*Hermeneutik und Ideologiekritik*, 1971: 129–31).

Further, systematically distorted communication as found individually in a neurotic person or socially in ideology cannot be interpreted by any simple hermeneutical procedure, but requires an explanatory understanding, which deploys a scientific theory of communication and society. Hence both psychoanalysis and critique of ideology take us beyond the framework of tradition and hermeneutics.

Already in his basic account of knowledge, Habermas had distinguished the knowledge reached by the empirical–analytic sciences and that of the hermeneutic–historical disciplines as two irreducible 'types of knowledge, corresponding to the two different cognitive interests, namely the technical and the practical.

In his separation of empirical science from hermeneutics Habermas falls behind the post-empiricistic analyses of science, which stress the interpretative element present in all the empirical sciences. Charles Taylor (1971), for example, argues that a purely empirical social science has to omit considerations of intersubjective and common meanings, which constitute the very social reality it claims to be studying. Social sciences must, he maintains, be hermeneutical if they are to be proportionate to their object. Compare that with Habermas's contention that the social media of work and domination (understood as the institutions controlling and legitimating power) are infralinguistic factors. Mary Hesse gives reasons for a continuity not a dichotomy between Habermas's model of the natural sciences and the hermeneutic model of the human sciences. She further argues against separating the natural sciences from the human sciences:

the understanding of man implies an understanding of related biological nature, and conversely. It is impossible in studying theories of evolution, ecology, or genetics, to separate a mode of knowledge relating to technical control from a mode relating to the self-understanding of man. This is not just to assert that human values will be involved in *applications* of these theories, though that is true too; it is also, and more centrally for the present discussion, to assert that the very categories of these theories, such as functionality, selection, survival, are infected by man's view of himself (1972: 292 – Hesse's italics).

Again:

theories have always been expressive of the myth or metaphysics of a society, and have therefore been part of the internal communication of that society. Society interprets itself to itself partly by means of its view of nature (*ibid.*).

Even in regard to the natural sciences, it is therefore doubtful whether the irreducible distinction Habermas makes between the empirical–analytical sciences and the hermeneutic–historical disciplines can be sustained.

In a recent study on *Interests and the Growth of Knowledge*, Barry Barnes observes:

All knowledge is made by men from existing cultural resources; old knowledge is part of the raw material involved in the manufacture of new; hence, whatever the interests which guide knowledge generation, socially sustained consensus and a modification of existing meanings will always be involved in the process. Habermas, like Lukács, ignores this essential connection of scientific knowledge with its cultural antecedents, and this constitutes the crucial formal inadequacy in his account, the central misconception to which all else can be related. This is why Habermas does not realise that in describing 'hermeneutic' knowledge, he is merely pointing out certain universal features of all knowledge (1977: 18).

Habermas gives a wide extension to the empirical–analytic mode of knowledge. The social sciences in their nomological function are empirical–analytic sciences. A critical theory of communication and society will be empirical–analytic. The reconstructive sciences would seem to belong to the same general mode of knowledge, despite their reflective character. And discourse, with its suspension or virtualization of action, is conceived as impersonal, objective or theoretical argumentation. Even 'practical discourse', which is 'practical' in the sense of being concerned with the norms governing human affairs as distinct from 'technical' as concerned with physical laws, belongs to theory, because it is the 'theoretical justification' of norms (1973b: 254).

We are reminded here of the great stress the Marxist tradition lays upon reason and the great confidence it has in scientific reason for the analysis and solution of the problems of human society. Despite his opposition to positivism and his critique of positivistic tendencies in Marx himself, Habermas continues the Marxist tradition in elaborating scientific rational procedures for enlightenment and for the organization of an emancipated order of society. The question is whether reason in its functioning in human affairs is still conceived here too narrowly, because theoretical science remains the ideal.

Most people took Habermas's account of the relation between knowledge and human interests as curbing the pretensions of theory to be free from the constraints of action. Yet, in his more recent writing he sets up as an ideal a speech situation in which any link with action is suspended. No doubt, he still acknowledges the dialectic between theory and *praxis* in so far as he repeatedly asserts that the ideal speech situation can be realized only when concrete social conditions are free from domination. Nevertheless, his concept of discourse assumes that the pressure of action is an obstacle not an aid to truth, so that truth is grounded and norms justified only in a discourse where the demands of action are suspended. In my opinion he makes an over-sharp distinction between discourse and action, stating, I think with much exaggeration, that in the realm of action validity claims are uncritically accepted (1973a: 168). In fact, there is a continuity such that the boundaries are blurred. A critical examination of disputed claims can well be pursued in and through chosen courses of action, and the holding of set discourse may be a noteworthy political action.

Detached discourse can only be carried on by those who are already leading a moderately contented existence. It has a limited context and function. It cannot bring salvation to the human race locked in institutionalized unreason and unfreedom. Discourse draws the map of our journey to emancipation. It does not set our destination, nor provide the vehicle and motive power. Whenever men and women have been led to turn away from unreason and unfreedom, it has not been by detached discourse, but by experiences and insights that come like gifts, so that their recipients feel that they have been newly created by a power greater than themselves. While Habermas acknowledges the role of *praxis*, his steady conviction that religion is irretrievably obsolete and his Marxist emphasis upon reason and the rationally grounded close him to an appreciation of the gratuitous, unexpected, unaccountable character of human liberation: in brief, to that whole dimension summed up in the theological concept of grace. I for one cannot resist the impression that when by rational analysis Habermas finds freedom, justice and equality implicit in the speech situation, he is finding there what he brings from his own participation in the Western tradition. Outside the context of an emancipatory tradition, no rational analysis would of itself discover the emancipatory values, and any concepts thus reached would without tradition remain largely empty of concrete content.

Tradition can be and often has been a Babylonian captivity, because it has served as a pretext for the imposition and continuance of heteronomous authority. But it is also the irreplaceable repository of experiences too rich for discursive reason adequately to objectify and lay hold of. In making its claims it offers a transforming self-validation to participants. Freedom of discourse and the authority of tradition are not opposed, because reason, when not limited to formal reason, and freedom are not fixed endowments, but the result of a transformation of the human subject. Tradition is the author of such transformation, since it is the presence of the Spirit in human history.

5

Religion and the critique of domination

When I speak of critical theology, I am not using the word 'critical' as a vague expression of approval. As used here the word does indeed mean that any worthwhile theology should question its assumptions and not be the parroting of an unexamined tradition. It implies, too, that reason in theology as elsewhere is critical as having a negative function in dissolving habitual but inadequate modes of thought and action. But something more precise than all this is intended. The phrase 'critical theology' points to an attempt to link Christian theology to the tradition of criticism in Western culture, which goes back to the Enlightenment, passes through the critical philosophy of Kant, Fichte and Hegel to the Marxist critique of ideology and is represented most clearly today by the critical theory of society of the Frankfurt School. The link with that tradition is one of the concerns of the 'political theology' of Metz.

A preliminary task is to determine the meaning of 'critical' historically by giving some account of the emergence and development of criticism or the critical tradition.

The group of words represented by 'critique' in French and 'criticks', later 'criticism', in English came into these vernacular languages from Latin around the year 1600 (Koselleck, 1959: 81–103). (The word-group came later into German, being first found in the eighteenth century.) During the seventeenth century the words became naturalized in French and English. They were used to mean the art of sound judgement, especially with reference to the study of ancient texts. Criticism, therefore, expressly so called, began with the philological critique of traditional documents. The words, however, were quickly extended to embrace the aesthetic criticism of literature and art; and persons also became the object of criticism.

No opposition was at first felt between religion and criticism in the sense of philology, even when the sharpening philological methods were applied to the Bible. One could be Christian and critical at the same time, and to speak of learned and critical Christians was not incongruous. So much so, that the term 'criticaster' was invented for an unbelieving critic, Spinoza being dubbed 'some Jewish criticaster' (Koselleck, 1959: 191).

When in 1678 Richard Simon published his *Histoire critique du Vieux Testament*, he made a point in his preface of his use of 'critique' and the cognate words. These were technical words, familiar to scholars, and he refers to Louis Cappelle and his *Critica Sacra* (1650), the Calvinist to whom he owed the method and the words. These words were now being brought before a wider public. Simon wrote in French not in Latin.

Ironically, the innovating force of Simon's critical method may best be seen from the polemical use he makes of it to defend the Catholic faith against the Protestants. Criticism for Simon brings to light the vicissitudes to which the Biblical texts had been subject: the changes suffered in the course of time, the superimposed layers, the elements added later, the fitting together of pieces of different date and by different hand. All this, Simon argues, shows the impossibility of taking a stand upon Scripture alone and proves the Catholic position on the need for Church tradition. But the give-away comes when Simon insists that Protestants have to submit to the results of criticism, because the rules of the critical method are 'claires et évidentes' and thus independent of revelation. Criticism recognizes no theological *a priori*. No authority can make a text other than what it is, and the principles of criticism remain the same whether the text is sacred or profane. Simon, then, will not allow Protestants to evade the findings of criticism by any appeal to faith or theology. The work of the critic must be independent of theology and rest simply upon the clear and evident rules of philology. But if that is so, Catholics likewise must submit to the sovereignty of criticism, and with a consistency that undermines his polemical position against the Protestants, Simon is prepared to apply the critical method to the writings of tradition.

Simon was led one day to burn all his voluminous notes. For that reason we have no means of knowing his innermost faith

Theology and political society

or of following any inward struggles he might have had. Granted, however, that he sincerely wanted to put the new art of criticism at the service of his Church, we have to say that in fact he missed the revolutionary implications of the critical method as he understood and used it. In effect, his criticism removed the criterion of truth from revelation and authority and placed it in sound reasoning. If a dogma contradicts philology, then the dogma has to yield, not philology, which proceeds by the clear and evident rules of the critical method.

Other Catholics were more clear-sighted about what was at stake, and Simon met with condemnation from Church and State (Hazard, 1973: 213–31).

It was Bossuet who took steps to secure the banning of Simon's book, and in so many respects Bossuet was personally the antithesis of Richard Simon. Nevertheless, the conflict was more than personal. 'Bossuet at Bay' (*ibid.*, 232) was representative of Christian believers as they reacted defensively and undiscriminatingly to the advance of unbelief and critical thought. The brief harmony of criticism and Christian faith was over. Criticism now took on a negative relationship to religion, which became constitutive of the very concept of criticism in the eighteenth century.

Pierre Bayle in his *Dictionnaire historique et critique* of 1695, on which the eighteenth century drew heavily, gave criticism a generally negative meaning. He tells in a letter how he 'conceived the idea of compiling a critical dictionary, i.e. a dictionary which should comprise a complete inventory, as it were, of the various errors perpetrated, not only by lexicographers, but by writers in general' (*ibid.*, 131). But the negative stance of Bayle became a matter of principle where religion was concerned. For Bayle criticism did not merely imply or provoke a conflict with revelation, but was the very activity that established a realm of reason over against that of revelation. With the rise of criticism there thus emerges with a new intensity the old opposition between reason and revelation. Criticism and revelation repel each other as opposites.

'Criticism' became the catchword of the eighteenth century. Innumerable books and articles appeared with 'criticism' or 'critical' in their titles. It was the age of criticism, and people had the consciousness that theirs was a critical age.

As it swept through the age of Enlightenment, criticism was not limited to philology nor to aesthetics and history. It had become quite generally the art of rational thought or sound judgement in every sphere of theory and practice. Criticism was now synonymous with reason, but with reason understood in a particular way, not as the defence or contemplative representation of a luminous cosmic order, but as an endless struggle for an always imperfectly grasped truth. Critical reason was the energy that restlessly drives argument onwards, ceaselessly weighing the pros and cons of every position. Rational thought as critical questioned everything; it was a never-ending and relativizing process.

A culmination was reached when criticism turned back upon reason itself. This took place in the so-called critical turn of Kant when criticism now reflected upon the antinomies of reason and then proceeded to set out the limits and preconditions of knowledge.

But before we consider the passage of criticism into critical philosophy, more must be said about the features and movement of criticism in the eighteenth century.

During the first half of that century, the conflict between critical reason and revelation held the front of the stage, but from the middle of the century onwards the conviction was widespread that revealed religion had been overcome and that revelation was no longer an issue. Criticism increasingly turned its attention to the State and became political criticism.

The context for the rise of political criticism was the Absolute State. As a political system the Absolute State was a result of the Religious Wars. These were brought to an end by separating politics from religion and morality. Hence the Absolute State was constructed upon the basis of a dualism. A sphere of absolute, sovereign power was carved out for the State by limiting the function of moral and religious conscience to an apolitical inner realm. This dualism is very plain in Bayle. When for him criticism laid claim to complete freedom, it did so only in 'La République de Lettres', a sphere marked off clearly from that of the State. A distinction was made between men as subjects and men as men. Criticism belonged to the private, inner realm, which the State had to concede to men as men, while exerting absolute power over them as subjects. Thus, for Bayle, criticism was consciously apolitical as not touching the State as State. Voltaire still maintains the apolitical character of criticism, but he does so now with irony and as a tactic, while clearly conscious of the *de facto* political nature of criticism. Not all his successors, however, showed the same awareness of what they were doing. There was an illusion of detachment or political neutrality, which distorted the relation of criticism in its bourgeois form to society and tradition.

By the time of Kant there was indeed an open assertion of the rights of criticism over the State. In the Preface to the first edition of the *Critique of Pure Reason* Kant writes:

Our age is, in especial degree, the age of criticism, and to criticism everything must submit. Religion through its sanctity, and law-giving through its majesty may seek to exempt themselves from it. But they then awaken just suspicion, and cannot claim the sincere respect which reason accords only to that which has been able to sustain the test of free and open examination (1965: 9).

Criticism, therefore, which originated and developed in the private inner realm left by the absolutist political system to its subjects as men, moved from philological and aesthetic beginnings through a critique of religion and the supposedly apolitical–political criticism of Bayle and Voltaire to overt political criticism. Nevertheless, the dualistic context of its origins continued to affect criticism, creating a false consciousness about its political function.

Socially and politically criticism represented the emergence of a new ruling class, namely the bourgeoisie. When the absolutist system separated off an apolitical, autonomous, private realm, in order to clear a space for its own absolute power, it sowed the seeds of its own destruction. Unwittingly it allowed the growth of a political consciousness and criticism set loose from the restraints of a traditional social system. The consequences were fateful. Intellectually, the criticism of the Enlightenment repudiated all tradition and set up an opposition between reason and tradition that broke the continuity of Western culture. Politically, criticism resulted in the French Revolution and the eventual destruction of the old order in

Europe. Despite that, the bearers of the new political order did not acknowledge their thought or criticism as the expression of the social and political aspirations of their class. Instead, they put forward their critique as a detached, neutral, objective pursuit of truth. They concealed their own social and political role. Thus, the depoliticization of intelligence and society, namely the illusory denial of the political or power implications of intellectual and socio-economic activities, became constitutive of bourgeois society. The result was the proliferation of a theoretical knowledge without a reflexive relationship to human social action or practice, and consequently objectivistic and individualistic in its structure and amoral in its use.

The same point may be expressed as the evasion of the link that binds criticism to crisis. Both words go back to the Greek *krinō*, but not until the nineteenth century is criticism explicitly related to crisis. The bearing of the loss of that relationship may be seen by comparison with Greek usage. In the Greek juridical use of *krinō* and *krisis*, the judgement was understood as an element within the *krisis*, which was interpreted as the entire process or struggle towards a decision. The crisis was an objective whole, of which the judgement or critique was a part. On the contrary, for the Enlightenment criticism was a subjective activity or faculty, placed outside the context of an objective crisis or process. History was conceived as a progress towards criticism rather than as itself a self-critical process, that is, as a crisis (Habermas, 1974a: 213).

The link between criticism and crisis was re-established in the nineteenth century, notably in Hegel and Marx, both of whom in their different ways presented world-history as a crisis complex.

Hegel, unlike the Young Hegelians after him, did not make frequent use of the word 'criticism' and its cognates. All the same, his contribution to the critical tradition has been fundamental.

As a student at the theological *Stift* at Tübingen, Hegel did not at first pay much attention to the discussions then surrounding the critical philosophy of Kant. But during 1792 and 1793 two events aroused the interest of the Tübingen students, including Hegel, in the moral and religious philosophy of Kant and Fichte. These events were the publication of Kant's essay, 'On the radical evil in human nature', in the *Berlinische Monatsschrift* for February 1792 and a visit of Fichte to Tübingen in June 1793. Kant's article became part of *Religion Within the Limits of Reason Alone*, which came out in 1793. Fichte had published his *Essay Toward a Critique of All Revelation* at Easter 1792 and had acknowledged its authorship in the autumn of that year. In the discussions that ensued over these writings at the *Stift* a conflict emerged between a moderate group, trying to use them to support Lutheran orthodoxy, and a radical group, pressing their critical implications. Hegel's sympathies were with the latter (Harris, 1972: 107–19).

The influence of the moral philosophy of Kant is evident in Hegel's early writing, *The Life of Jesus* (1795), which comes from his period at Berne as a family tutor. He quickly moved, however, beyond Kantian moralism, as is already manifest in *The Spirit of Christianity and Its Fate* (1800), another early writing, this time from his stay, again as a tutor, at Frankfurt.

Hegel did not confine his interest to the moral and religious questions raised by critical philosophy, but passed on from them to the theoretical issues. The first-fruits of his thinking are to be found in the writings and lectures composed after he had moved to the University of Jena in 1801. This was the period of his collaboration with Schelling, but also of the emergence of his own independent system. As is well known, he contributed to the discussions of critical philosophy by his first book, *Difference between the Philosophical Systems of Fichte and Schelling* (1801), and by an article, 'Faith and knowledge', a critique of Kant, Jacobi and Fichte, which appeared in the *Kritisches Journal*, edited by himself and Schelling. Less notice has been given to the programmatic essay Hegel wrote for the first number of that *Journal* (1802), entitled 'On the nature of philosophical criticism in general and its relationship to the present state of philosophy in particular' (*Über das Wesen der philosophischen Kritik überhaupt, und ihr Verhältnis zum gegenwärtigen Zustand der Philosophie insbesondere*) (Hegel, 1968: 117–28). His analysis here of the meaning of criticism helps us to grasp the reasons why he was able to regard his own highly metaphysical philosophy as genuinely critical.

In the essay Hegel sharply distinguishes between criticism

and party strife, which is merely the endless clash of subjectivity with subjectivity. For there to be criticism, the Idea of philosophy must be present. Philosophy is always one and the same, despite differences of form, and there must be a presence of its Idea in all the participants in criticism. Further, only those works which express the Idea, even if more or less clearly, can be brought under criticism. What Hegel calls *Unphilosophie*, namely writings or theories that do not contain the Idea of philosophy, cannot be criticized in the proper sense. 'All criticism is subsumption under the Idea; where that is lacking, all criticism necessarily ceases' (*ibid.*, 118).

Criticism supposes the truth of reason and the possibility of knowledge of reality. Otherwise, there would be no objectivity of judgement. The role of criticism is to take up the different forms in which the Idea of philosophy comes to expression, in order to break open their limitations and thus prepare the way for a scientific system of philosophy.

That presentation of criticism as a process within the Idea of philosophy anticipates the dialectical movement set forth in Hegel's major writings. In the Hegelian dialectic the negation or critical moment is a determinate negation, which is then sublated into a synthesis. In other words, criticism for Hegel is always immanent criticism, where the negation is determinate in so far as it presupposes the presence of the Idea in what is criticized.

We may take a closer look at Hegel's own contribution to critical philosophy by briefly considering his critique of Kant and his rejection of Kant's epistemological approach to the function of criticism. In Kant, as we have seen, the development of criticism reached a turning-point, because with him criticism became reflection upon reason itself. Philosophy became critical philosophy. Philosophical critique in the Kantian sense was reflection upon the transcendental conditions of knowledge. It changed the relationship of subject and object. The phenomenal world was no longer imposed upon the subject by the object, but constructed by the subject. Philosophy became reflective in making the subject aware that the object was a construct. There is an emancipatory thrust in Kant's epistemology in as much as for it the ordered world is a product of the spontaneity of the human spirit, instead of a pre-given reality. But Kant himself did not fully recognize this, and he gave the categories he uncovered an uncritical necessity.

Hegel in any event rejected Kant's epistemology. No prior critique of knowing, he argued, could establish the validity of knowledge, because any criteria or pre-conditions of knowledge such a critique may specify are already known. The investigation of the faculty of knowing is itself knowledge, and therefore cannot justify knowledge. Epistemology is a circular argument, because it has to claim as knowledge the criteria it proposes for knowledge. It seeks to know before we know, which is as absurd, Hegel quips, as wanting to swim before venturing into the water (1975a: 14).

For Hegel phenomenological reflection upon the formation of consciousness replaces epistemology. Instead of seeking and claiming an indubitable starting-point, phenomenology in Hegel begins with the data of ordinary consciousness taken uncritically. It then institutes a process of historico-genetic reflection, which reconstructs the self-formation of consciousness and shows how at every stage in the sequence of states of consciousness the criteria of the preceding stage break down and new criteria arise. The progress through the successive stages of knowledge is a critical process, because of the negation that dissolves each form of consciousness and gives rise to a new form. The negation is a determinate negation in the sense that it is a negation of that from which it results and as such always has a positive content. The old form of consciousness gives rise to the succeeding form. Hence the negativity of the dialectical or critical process is not the empty or abstract negativity of scepticism. The road it follows is a more radical one than that of simple doubt. Phenomenological reflection, as Hegel remarks in the Introduction to *The Phenomenology of Spirit* (1975c: 72), is not a pathway of doubt (*Zweifel*), but, more properly, a highway of despair (*Verzweiflung*). Doubt is a questioning of a particular truth, which is usually followed by a return to that truth after the doubt has been dispelled. Even the total sceptic is imprisoned within a particular form of consciousness, which should yield to a subsequent form just as it itself is the outcome of a preceding one. Phenomenological reflection, unlike doubt, is a highway of despair, because it brings an insight into the untruth of all incomplete forms of consciousness before the goal of absolute knowledge is reached.

The progression from one form of consciousness to the next embraces not only the object but the subject. Subject and object remain correlative throughout, and phenomenology is thus the reconstruction of the self-formation of the subject. Hegel, therefore, rejects the Kantian concept of the ego as a fixed knowing subject. Further, the formation of the individual is seen as a socialization. Self-consciousness is an awareness of self through the other. The phenomenology opens up upon society and indeed upon the universal history of mankind. Thus the critique of knowledge cannot be separated from the critique of action. The Kantian distinction between theoretical and practical reason is rejected. Critical consciousness emerges from an historical development that dissolves alienated forms of life. In brief, Hegel's critical philosophy as phenomenological reflection was a reconstruction of the dialectical process of world-history. Because the process was dialectical, world-history was seen as a crisis complex, each successive stage being negated and yet, since the negation was a determinate negation, being retained in the higher stage of the totality.

Hegel's critical philosophy is also an ontology. The world is posited by Spirit, whose essence is rational necessity.

The philosophy of Kant represents the Enlightenment aspiration towards autonomy. It views men as subjects with a self-defining identity. Men are no longer defined heteronomously in relation to a cosmic order, but as constructing their own world and possessing a rational, self-legislating freedom. The counterpart of this concept of the autonomous self was a view of nature as neutral, contingent fact, an objectified order to be mapped and then manipulated. The physical sciences were for Kant prototypical knowledge. In the interpretation of Charles Taylor (1975: 3–50), Hegel set out to combine the Enlightenment concept of the free and self-defining subject with the expressivist trend of thought. Expressivism is the reaction, begun in Herder and Rousseau and continued in the Romantics, against the objectification of the world and the self. It insisted upon an organic relation of men, society, nature, social institutions and culture, all joined in a unity of meaningful expression. Hegel, Taylor argues, took up this expressivist theory in making nature and history expressions of the Spirit. What distinguished Hegel from the Romantics was his emphasis upon reason and the rational. The life of the Spirit is rational thought, which is expressed in our own thought in so far as we think rationally, and is embodied in the world and history as the rational necessity of its structure and unfolding.

Marx condemned Hegel's philosophy as insufficiently critical. He speaks of Hegel's 'merely apparent criticism' (Colletti, ed., 1975: 393) and, while he accepted from the *Phenomenology* 'the dialectic of negativity as the moving and producing principle' (*ibid.*, 386), Marx argued that:

In Hegel, therefore, the negation of the negation is not the confirmation of true being through the negation of apparent being. It is the confirmation of apparent being or self-estranged being in its negation, or the negation of this apparent being as an objective being residing outside man and independent of him and its transformation into the subject (*ibid.*, 393).

Behind this critique of Hegel's dialectic as uncritical lies Marx's rejection of Hegel's idealism with its thesis on the Spirit and on the ultimate identity of subject and object. The subject of the dialectical process of world-history is, for Marx, not the Spirit, but the concrete species of man, reproducing its life in a relationship with nature through social labour.

Already the Young Hegelians, chiefly the three Bauer brothers, Stirner and Strauss, had anthropologized Hegel's dialectic, transferring it from the Spirit to the free self-consciousness of man. In doing so, they exalted the principle of criticism and made it the one method of arriving at truth and preparing for the emergence of humanism. Because in its dialectical unfolding human self-consciousness proceeded by negating each of its forms, it advanced by criticism. Criticism was thus the negative principle necessary for progress. All outmoded forms were to be rejected.

The Young Hegelians turned their critical attack first against traditional religious forms. They saw all religion, including

Christianity, as myth, a thesis presented in Strauss's *Life of Jesus* in 1835, which adopted criticism as its method. It was natural that the Young Hegelian criticism should thus first be theological. An interest in religion was part of Hegel's legacy and, because of the attitude of the Prussian government, it was a much safer area than politics. Nevertheless, criticism soon moved to politics and society. The outlook of the Young Hegelians remained, however, idealist. They disdained the empirical approach and exalted theory. Bruno Bauer described criticism as 'the terrorism of pure theory' (Brazill, 1970: 80). It was theoretical criticism to which outmoded institutions were expected to succumb and thus yield to a humanist order. This was where Marx differed and separated himself from the Young Hegelians. In 1844 he decided with Engels to dispose of Bruno Bauer in *The Holy Family* (a reference to the Bauer brothers), subtitled 'Critique of Critical Criticism'. 'Ideas', he writes there, 'never lead beyond the established situation, they only lead beyond the ideas of the established situation. Ideas can accomplish absolutely nothing. To become real, ideas require men who apply practical force' (McLellan, 1973: 134).

In the spring of the following year, 1845, Marx wrote his *Theses on Feuerbach*, of which the eleventh reads: 'The philosophers have only *interpreted* the world, in various ways; the point is to *change* it' (Colletti, ed., 1975: 423 – Marx's italics). Marx was able to write that, because he had completed the anthropologizing of Hegel's synthesis. The subject of world-history is not the Spirit, as Hegel maintained, not human self-consciousness as Bauer held, not the abstract human essence or even material man but as an object of contemplation, which is Feuerbach's view in Marx's interpretation. The subject of history is flesh-and-blood men actively related to nature through social labour. At the basic level, then, there is the process of productive labour as the interrelationship and interaction of men with nature. Through this process, men make nature into an expression of themselves and at the same time become properly men or create themselves. But this occurs only through conflict and division. In developing themselves through labour, men initiate modes of production that bring the exploitation and alienations of a class society. Men thus divided over against one another cannot achieve an adequate expression of themselves. Once, however, a sufficient mastery over nature has been reached in the process of production, men can overcome their divisions and the various forms of alienation and enter into a realm of freedom and reconciliation.

Marx thus presented world-history as a crisis complex, namely an objectively critical or dialectical process, but now conceived materialistically in terms of production or social labour. He saw his theoretical work or critique as an element in that crisis. A crisis is when the contradictions inherent in a situation or system culminate in a turning-point and demand a resolution so as to effect the liberation of those involved. At the beginning of bourgeois society the emancipatory process was carried forward so powerfully and easily that, as I have already noted, the sense of a link between critique and crisis was lost, so that bourgeois critique was conceived simply as a subjective activity. In Marx, on the contrary, critique is now firmly related to the objective crises of industrial capitalist society.

There are two meanings present when Marx refers to his investigation of capitalist society as critique. First, he examines capitalist society by a critique of the reflection of that society in the texts of the bourgeois science of political economy. In other words, for him critique was a critique of ideology, the uncovering of the concealed interests and social domination embodied in current theory. Second, at the same time, he put forward a theory developed with the practical intention of overcoming the crisis, a theory intended to bring to consciousness the dialectic of history and serve as the theoretical counterpart of a revolutionary *praxis*. Critique also meant the critical theory known as historical materialism.

Critique for Marx superseded philosophy; it was both the abolition and the realization at a higher level, that is, the *Aufhebung*, of philosophy. Bourgeois philosophy was idealist; it started with thought and tried to arrive at being. It sought the reconciliation of man and the world simply in reinterpreting the world. The primacy it thus gave to theory sprang from its reduction of concrete men to consciousness or thought, and this reduction in its turn was rooted in the political and social fact that any attempt to reform social life had been abandoned. The solution of the contradictions of society was placed in thought, not in being. No total philosophy, Marx saw, could be critical, because by it every element is integrated into the whole, and one cannot alter the universe. With his critique, Marx turned away from metaphysics or First Philosophy and established a new unity of theory and practice. He rejected the notion of theory as independent of practice, that is, theory as a contemplative recognition of a stable object. Theory becomes now the consciousness of practice, the reflective element of social activity and, as distinct from ideology, inseparable from the concrete historical effort to overcome the contradictions of existing society (Davis, 1973; Habermas, 1971a: 11–36).

What however became dominant in modern Western culture was neither critical philosophy nor Marxist critique, but positivism. Positivism is the refusal of reflection, and its dominance corresponds to the industrial, technological and rationalized civilization of the nineteenth and twentieth centuries, which objectifies and instrumentalizes, not just nature, but men in their social relations and practices (Taylor, 1975: 540–6). Positivism rejects the Kantian demand for transcendental reflection upon the limits and conditions of knowledge. The objectivity of knowledge is secured, not by reflection, but by empirical observation when under intersubjective control. No critical justification is given for the scientistic claim that identifies knowledge with empirical science. Epistemology is replaced by philosophy of science, which simply articulates established procedures of research. Hegel was rejected because of his ontology. Marx was reproached for having confused fact and value.

When, therefore, in the 1930s Max Horkheimer, in collaboration with Adorno and other members of the Frankfurt Institute for Social Research, developed his Critical Theory of society, he did so in opposition to bourgeois science, particularly social science, and its positivism. His opposition to positivism has been continued by Habermas (1972b; Adorno *et al.*, 1976) and Wellmer (1974) of the younger generation of the Frankfurt School. The Critical Theory is thus Hegelian in as much as like Hegel it endeavours to combine an expressivist protest against the mechanistic concept of man and nature, coming from a onesided development of instrumental reason in the main trend of the Enlightenment, with an acceptance of Enlightenment emancipation and the ideal of autonomous reason and freedom. The Critical Theory is also Marxist. It originated among German Marxists and falls within the general context of a Marxist interpretation of society and history. At the same time, it has developed a critique of the latent positivism of Marx himself and has worked to correct the defects in Marx's thought that have led to the destructive dominance of technical and bureaucratic rationality within official Marxism.

There are two related points in the Frankfurt School's criticism of Marx. The first is the inadequacy of Marx's conceptualization of human action. For Marx the paradigm of human action was labour or material production. While in conceiving this as social labour, he implicitly acknowledged its context of communicative action, he did not explicitly articulate the distinction between labour and social interaction as two irreducible forms of human action. He therefore tended to reduce *praxis* to *techne* or instrumental action. The second point concerns the deterministic element in Marx's philosophy of history. He held that the development of capitalist society would lead to a revolutionary situation. He envisaged the progress of science and technology as bringing mastery over nature and an advance in productive forces, and thus creating the material conditions for the transition to an emancipated or classless society. But he assumed that the material conditions are sufficient conditions, neglected the subjective conditions required for the self-emancipation of the proletariat and, in particular, overlooked the stultifying impact of scientific and technological progress upon the consciousness of the potential subjects of revolution. He did not anticipate the technocratic consciousness of one-dimensional man.

The writings of Horkheimer and Adorno represent a shift from the critique of political economy to a critique of instrumental reason and its positivistic results, together with the introduction of a wide-ranging socio-cultural analysis into Marxist social theory. Habermas continues their critique of positivism and shares the desire of his elders to correct and complement Marx. But, as Wellmer puts it, his intention of criticizing science is joined with that of making criticism scientific' (1974: 137). He attempts to go beyond the pessimistic *Kulturkritik* of the Frankfurt School to a comprehensive and systematic theory of human action and of society, which would embrace the economic, political and socio-cultural elements of society, complementing and correcting Marx, while retaining the fundamental assumptions of historical materialism.[16]

We may now briefly retrace our steps. The modern critique of Western culture began with the philological criticism of the documents of its tradition. It continued with the criticism of its religious and political institutions in the name of reason and freedom in the eighteenth century. With Kant and German idealism it became a process of philosophical reflection, which may be seen as an attempt to thematize theoretically the changes involved in the transition from traditional to modern society. In Marx theoretical analysis was animated with a practical intent and made the consciousness of a revolutionary practice. But the immediate future did not lie with the transformation of capitalist society into a communist, classless society, but to an increasingly technological and bureaucratic society, with the dominance of instrumental reason.

This society embodies the autonomous reason and negative freedom of the early Enlightenment, and those who are at home in modern society with its empiricism and possessive individualism belong to that Enlightenment tradition. The attempt of Hegel, followed in that respect by Marx, to combine adherence to Enlightenment emancipation with a protest against the onesidedness of its original conception and the alienation that onesidedness has produced is continued in the Critical Theory of the Frankfurt School. Hence its attraction for those who experience our present society as profoundly unsatisfactory and yet do not wish to fall into a protesting irrationalism, whether of the activist or the mystical variety.

But how does religion relate to that now long-standing critical tradition?

The eighteenth-century Enlightenment rejected revealed religion and ecclesiastical authority as heteronomous. Traditional religion and secular intelligence came into an open antagonism. Kant, however, moved beyond that. Though a man of the Enlightenment in embracing the autonomy of reason and rejecting dogmatism, he did not see any opposition in principle between the secular and the religious. He laid down limits for theoretical reason, in order to make room for faith. He established a rational faith upon practical reason, that is, upon human free moral agency. He reinterpreted Christianity to fit into the framework of his conception of the human being as a self-legislating rational moral subject. He did not deny the idea of a special divine revelation, but claimed the right of a philosophical critique of such revelation, using his basic moral conception of religion as a criterion.

But Kant's moral interpretation of Christianity proved too restrictive. Further, his double dichotomy between phenomena and noumena and between theoretical and practical reason had the effect of isolating faith as private, thus depriving it of a public critical function in society. Kant's account of human subjectivity left it awkwardly straddling the phenomenal and noumenal orders. In its phenomenal expressions and its progressive realization in history, it came under empirical investigation and theoretical reason. Nevertheless, the human self with its freedom, its moral imperatives and its regulative ideas belonged essentially to the noumenal order. It therefore transcended empirical investigation and theoretical reason. Because of that, the interests and values arising from freedom and faith were put apart from the realm of objective, scientific knowledge, which, through its technological and bureaucratic extensions, increasingly pervaded and controlled society.

Hegel's rejection of Kant's double dualism of phenomena and noumena and of theoretical and practical reason enabled him to put religion back into the world and history.

The Christian intention of Hegel's philosophy is now widely recognized. He set out to reconcile religious and secular consciousness, which had fallen apart into open conflict in modern society. He attempted to achieve the reconciliation through philosophy. We may say with Quentin Lauer that 'Hegel's has been a gigantic effort to rescue both Christian religion and philosophy by ultimately identifying them' (Christensen, ed., 1970: 275). Christianity as the absolute religion and philosophy as absolute knowledge have the same content. Philosophy gives that content its adequate form, while, on the other hand, only through religion can philosophy reach its object, absolute truth. The relation between philosophy and religion in Hegel is stated well by Emil Fackenheim:

> It is a central Hegelian doctrine that the true religion already is the true 'content', lacking merely the true 'form' of speculative thought; that philosophy could not reach truth unless its true content pre-existed in religion; that philosophical thought therefore requires religion as its basis in life, and that the true philosophy in giving the true religious content its true form of thought, both transfigures religion and produces itself (1967: 23).

On that interpretation, it is not true, as often thought, that philosophy for Hegel supersedes religion. Religion retains its autonomy, and the religious content does not cease to be religious when it has been conceptualized and thus given its adequate form by philosophy. Philosophy of religion for Hegel is not a philosophizing about religion, a philosophizing that remains itself apart from religion, but the thinking philosophically what religion thinks religiously.

All the same, it can be and has been questioned whether the transformed Christian God and the transformed Christian religion of Hegel's philosophical reconciliation of Christianity and Enlightenment remain truly Christian. Moreover, the Hegelian philosophical theology rests upon an ontology, now generally regarded with some reason today as untenable.

Despite the questionableness of his synthesis, Hegel does make, I think, an important contribution to our understanding of criticism as applied to religion. Since its emergence at the Enlightenment, critical reason has seemed of its very nature to be destructive of traditional religion, because implying the evaluation of revelation and faith from the outside. There is a dilemma here. To use external criteria to criticize faith is to subordinate faith to secular reason and thus to destroy it as faith. On the other hand, to refuse reason an independent critique of faith is irrational dogmatism. In other words, how can a person remain a believer after subjecting his faith to critique and, on the other hand, how can a person remain a philosopher if he continues to affirm a faith?

Now, as Quentin Lauer points out, 'Hegel need yield to none in his emphasis on the secular character of thought in the sense that he sees thought as thoroughly rooted in the autonomy of human spirit. He will accept no authority outside human thought as arbiter of that thought's validity. The rationality of thought and its autonomy are identified' (Christensen, ed., 1970: 261). But the dialectical and thus immanent character of Hegel's critique enabled him to avoid the dilemma I have sketched.

The dilemma of critical faith is parallel to the dilemma of Kantian epistemology, to which I have already given Hegel's answer. He argued that there can be no prior critique of knowing, because the criteria of any such critique are already knowledge. What one has to do is to begin with ordinary consciousness, initiating a process of phenomenological reflection, through which there is a transition from less adequate to more adequate stages of consciousness. An immanent critique pushes each stage of consciousness to the limits where it manifests its incompleteness and gives rise to a new stage. Likewise, the various forms of religious faith are criticized, not from without but from within. Self-reflection leads to the negation of each inadequate form and at the same time gives rise to the succeeding form. The negation of dialectical criticism is always a determinate negation, that is, a negation with a positive content.

Unlike rationalist and empiricist criticism, dialectical criticism acknowledges that there is no absolute starting-point. No Archimedean point can be found on which we can rest, neither the set of necessary, self-evident truths of the rationalists nor the sense-data of the empiricists. We move towards the absolute as critical reflection uncovers a lack of correspondence between subject and object at our existing stage of consciousness and leads to a higher formation of both subject and object. Rationalist and empiricist criticism destroys faith by subordinating it to some external criterion. Any critical theology or critique of faith, I should maintain, must be dialectical, so that criticism is identified with the dynamism of faith itself.

Although for Hegel himself religion did not lose its autonomy when conceptually transformed in philosophy, he did, as George Kline has noted, 'introduce into the history of Western philosophy the view of religion as a transition-form in the historical development of the human spirit' (Christensen, ed.,

1970: 192). He was, Kline continues, 'the first major European thinker – although Herder partially anticipated this view – to see religions as historical phenomena, phenomena that arise, flourish, and are superseded at specific times and in specific places' (*ibid.*). That theme was taken up by the Young Hegelians and interpreted as meaning that all religions, including Christianity, were defective and transitional, cancelled and superseded by philosophy.

Karl Marx came on the scene as a Young Hegelian, sharing their negation of religion. He soon moved away from them in his thinking as a whole. But did his view of religion remain unchanged? Despite all that has been written on the subject, it is even now difficult to assess Marx's critique of religion. The problem is that nearly everything Marx has to say about religion is to be found in his early writings, where religion is a prominent theme. In the writings of the mature Marx, the critique of religion recedes almost to nothing, so that in *Das Kapital* there are only scattered remarks. How are we to interpret that? Shall we echo Marx's own words in his most notable and most quoted treatment of religion, *A Contribution to the Critique of Hegel's Philosophy of Right: Introduction*, and say that for Marx already in 1843 at the age of twenty-five 'the criticism of religion has been essentially completed?' (Colletti, ed., 1975: 243). Most writers on Marx and religion do in effect do that, because what they in fact study is the statements of the young Marx. Or shall we look for some indication that Marx modified his critique of religion as his social thought in general developed? In doing so, we will have to recognize that the mature Marx left his work incomplete and suggested lines of thought he was not able to follow up himself. This is the view taken by Per Frostin (1978) in his recent study of Marx's critique of religion. Frostin in his interpretation gives central place to what he calls 'the forgotten text in *Das Kapital*', in which, contrary to his youthful statements that the critique of religion was completed, Marx points the way to a materialistic, which means a scientific, critique of religion scarcely yet begun, let alone finished.

I will outline the rejection of religion in the early Marx and then look at the text in *Das Kapital*, underlined by Frostin.

The youthful Marx's negation of religion was even more

unqualified than that of the other Young Hegelians. Religion was for him not just a transitional phenomenon, but an inverted consciousness, bound up with socio-economic exploitation and destined for annulment. Religion for Marx was alienated consciousness, in as much as it objectified human qualities, actions and potentialities, reified them as independent entities and thus constituted a consciousness divided against itself. But religion was more than one instance among others of alienation; it was alienation itself come to expression. The divisions and contradictions of the economic and political orders found their articulation in religion. Religion was nothing more than the mystifying formulation of the cleavages and false structures of unfree society. Emancipation, therefore, was identical with the end of religion.

Marx, therefore, identified religion with a false or mystified consciousness; or, in other words, religion was the same as ideology. He did not see religion as the cause or source of alienation; for him the Young Hegelians in doing so were still idealists. It is economic alienation that is basic. This has caused political alienation, which in its turn has generated religion. Religion is an epiphenomenon. As he wrote to Arnold Ruge: 'religion has no content of its own and lives not from heaven but from earth, and falls of itself with the dissolution of the inverted reality whose theory it is' (McLellan, 1973: 58).

Hence the need to go beyond Feuerbach, so that 'the criticism of heaven turns into the criticism of earth, the criticism of religion into the criticism of law and the criticism of theology into the criticism of politics' (Colletti, ed., 1975: 244–5).

Feuerbach had introduced the transformative method of interpreting the alienated consciousness of religion. He saw religious consciousness as an inversion of the true relationship between subject and predicate. Predicates or dependent realities were turned by religion into independent subjects as heavenly realities, while man, the true subject, lost his independent reality. The transformative method restored man and nature as the true subjects and reduced the heavenly realities of religion to their true status as predicates. For example, God is love means human love is divine, which further means man in his loving is of infinite worth. Marx extended Feuerbach's transformative method to political and economic relation-

124

ships. The State is not an independent, as it were heavenly, reality as Hegel presents it, but the creation or predicate of men in their concrete social relationships. Commodities are not the independent or mysterious realities they seem, but objectified human labour. Marx thus carried out the programme he had sketched in his fourth thesis on Feuerbach:

His work consists in resolving the religious world into its secular basis. But that the secular basis detaches itself from itself and establishes itself as an independent realm in the clouds can only be explained by the cleavages and self-contradictions within this secular basis. The latter must, therefore, in itself be both understood in its contradiction and revolutionized in practice (*ibid.*, 422).

Marx's early critique of religion may also be seen as the culmination of his critique of philosophy, that is, of Hegel. Theology or religion was for Marx the infected spot, the diseased element of philosophy. It was precisely in as much as it remained a theology that philosophy was ideology. What characterized thought as religious for Marx was its being mere theory divorced from social practice. By claiming permanent and universal truth in theory as if it were independent of social conditions, religion, and thus philosophy as religious, uncritically reflected patterns of social dominance and concealed social reality in mystifying abstractions. Philosophy itself, according to Marx, was to find a higher realization through its negation or abolition (*Aufhebung*) in a unity of theory and practice. Religion or theology could be given no such fulfilment. It is ideology through and through and is destined simply to disappear.

Such, in brief, is the view of religion as drawn from his early writings and usually attributed without further qualification to Marx as his critique of religion. But that critique can be dismissed on Marx's own principles as embodied in his mature work. First, unlike his critique of political economy, Marx's critique of religion does not rest upon a scientific analysis of the concrete data of religion, but is little more than a negative manner of asserting the ideal of an unalienated society. In short, it is a form of negative utopianism. Second, while in general Marx presents his theory of society as mediated through practice and therefore subject to development, modification, and in principle even to falsification, through the ongoing historical process, his theory of religion is asserted with a metaphysical absoluteness. His account of religion is thus self-contradictory, in as much as it rejects religion on the grounds that religion is pure theory independent of practice, but does so in a purely theoretical manner, disallowing the possible modification of the rejection by future practice.

Since we should not assume inconsistency in an author except as a last resort in interpretation, we are obliged to comb Marx's later writings for any hint that he recognized the need for a properly scientific critique of religion. Frostin considers he has discovered this in 'the forgotten text in *Das Kapital*'. 'The forgotten text' is a long footnote in chapter 13 of volume I. This footnote, according to Frostin (1978: 30), is the only place where the mature Marx deals with the principles and method of the critique of religion.

The general theme of the footnote is the need for a critical history of technology. Marx writes:

A critical history of technology would show how little any of the inventions of the eighteenth century were the work of one single individual. Hitherto, no such book has been published. Darwin has aroused our interest in the history of natural technology, that is to say in the origin of the organs of plants and animals as productive instruments utilised for the life purposes of these creatures. Does not the history of the origin of the productive organs of men in society, the organs which form the material basis of every kind of social organization, deserve equal attention? Since, as Vico says, the essence of the distinction between human history and natural history is that the former is the work of man and the latter is not, would not the history of human technology be easier to write than the history of natural technology? Technology reveals man's dealings with nature, discloses the direct productive activities of his life, thus throwing light upon social relations and the resultant mental conceptions.

Marx goes on immediately to apply the same principle to the history of religion:

Even the history of religion is uncritical unless this material basis be taken into account. Of course it is much easier, from an analysis of hazy constructions of religion, to discover their earthly core; than, conversely, to deduce from a study of the material conditions of life at any particular time, the celestial forms that these may assume. But the latter is the only materialistic method, and therefore the only scientific one. The abstract materialism of a natural science that excludes the historical process, is defective; as we can see in a moment when we glance at the abstract and ideological conceptions voiced by its advocates whenever they venture beyond the bounds of their own specialty (Marx, I, 1946: 392–3).

If now we follow Frostin's analysis, we find a threefold set of distinctions operative in that text. First, there is a distinction between two different types of the critique of religion: a materialistic and thus scientific type and another type that by way of contrast is clearly stigmatized as non-materialistic and non-scientific. Second, a distinction is drawn between two types of materialism, one that acknowledges history and originates the materialistic critique of religion and an abstract materialism that excludes the historical process, but which has validity within natural science, though not beyond its bounds. Third, natural history is distinguished from human history, the latter unlike the former being the work of man.

The footnote, therefore, shows that the mature Marx advocated a materialistic method, identified as scientific, which takes account of history as the work of man and thus as distinct from nature and rejected an abstract materialism that would extend the non-historical methods of the natural sciences to products of human history, such as religion.

What Marx describes as the materialistic and scientific critique of religion is said to begin with a study of the material conditions of life at each particular time, deducing the celestial forms these material conditions assumed in religious expression. A scientific critique of religion must therefore always rest upon a detailed study of the actual, concrete material conditions of life at every particular time and place. Consequently, any sweeping rejection of religion in general would seem to be excluded. The other type of critique of religion, a form of critique Marx now rejects, begins, the footnote tells us, from religious constructions themselves and analyses them to discover their earthly core; in other words, it takes religious ideas and reduces them to their secular basis.

Unmistakably, the description of the second type of critique applies to Feuerbach's anthropological interpretation of religion and to Marx's own critique of religion in his early writings. Despite, then, what many commentators say, Marx did not remain content with Feuerbach's critique of religion, merely urging its extension into a critique of earth, but came to regard it as methodologically mistaken. Since Marx's own early account of religion was in close correspondence with Feuerbach's, we may conclude with Frostin (1978: 15) that there is an essential difference between the early and the mature Marx in regard to the critique of religion.

The materialistic critique of the later Marx demands that religion should become an object of scientific investigation in the Marxist understanding of scientific method, namely that religious phenomena should be related in each case to the actual, concrete material conditions of life. The method, therefore, is to place religious phenomena in human history, materialistically conceived, and thus to relativize them. To put it with Frostin in another way: religion is for Marx a typical ideology and the critique of religion is simply a particular instance of the critique of ideology. Ideology for Marx was a set of general statements held and proclaimed in isolation from their historical basis. The purpose of the critique of ideology as such was not to prove the ideology false, but to uncover the hidden historical basis and thus to relativize its content. That was the programme for the critique of religion, adumbrated in the footnote in *Das Kapital*.

It was, however, only a programme, and nothing very much was done by Marx himself to execute it. It is true that Frostin manages to gather a handful of remarks from *Das Kapital*, which he sees with some reason as examples of the mature Marx's critique of religion, whereas others have seen in the passing references to religion in *Das Kapital* only 'sarcastic remarks' (Max Josef Suda in Mojzes, ed., 1978: 15). But even allowing full weight to the examples cited by Frostin, we have to admit that Marx through them and 'the forgotten text' merely points a direction, a direction which unfortunately was not followed by his disciples, who picked up instead and reaffirmed the earlier form of his critique of religion.

If, then, we agree to give 'the forgotten text' the immense significance Frostin gives it as establishing an essentially different critique of religion from that of Marx's early writings, wherein shall we place the challenge of that new critique to traditional religion? For Frostin the challenge simply coincides with the challenge of methodological atheism, which is the cornerstone of all modern science. The challenge is that, no more, no less. The materialism of Marx is not a new anti-theistic pseudo-religion, but simply a claim to investigate religious phenomena scientifically: that is, to offer an explanatory account of religion by seeking behind the phenomenal forms what is actually taking place in reality. The method is as Marx himself describes it in the Preface to the second edition of *Das Kapital*: 'The aim of investigation is to appropriate the matter in detail, to analyse its various developmental forms, and to trace the inner connexions between these forms. Not until this preliminary work has been effected, can the movement as it really is be suitably described' (Marx, II, 1946: 873). In other words, the aim is the description and explanation of the development or movement proper to social phenomena as historical. When applied to religion this method excludes, as all modern science does, any appeal to God and keeps therefore intact the principle of a methodological atheism. Hence for Frostin the challenge of Marx's critique is the same as the general challenge modern science makes to traditional religious understanding and theology. Marx claims that he has a scientifically better and more tenable explanation of religion than is to be found in the self-understanding of religion with its claims to a divine origin and a timeless validity. So, either Marx has overstepped the bounds of science with his claim or the Christian faith in its traditional self-understanding is unscientific.

Frostin himself does not in his published volume (two more are to follow) deal fully with the theological implications of the Marxist critique. For myself two lines of reflection suggest themselves.

The first concerns the self-understanding of religion as orthodoxy. One must say, I think, that the traditional conception of orthodoxy has been rendered untenable, so that, after Marx, there are not, in the words of Van Leeuwen, 'any real prospects of a radical renewal of theology except in the direction of what is sometimes defined as Politisches Theologie' (1972: 20).

According to the materialistic method of Marx, social and cultural phenomena are recognized as historical and as such the work of human beings. This is another way of insisting upon the unity between theory and practice, which destroys the structure of religion as an orthodoxy. Religion when maintained as an orthodoxy claims a permanent self-identity, remaining unscathed by social and practical changes. It invokes some purely theoretical centre of reference to serve in an abstract speculative way as a norm of identity. There are indeed conflicting orthodoxies, but the differences are conceived as basically theoretical. The presupposition of orthodoxy is the contemplative conception of knowledge, according to which knowledge is the result of the disinterested viewing of reality by individuals. Orthodoxy is that contemplative conception applied to religious truth. But for Marx knowledge is essentially a social product and is actively developed or changed in relation with practice. It is the consciousness or theoretical component of social action. In that sense, knowledge is mediated through concrete human history. We cannot anticipate that history. We possess the degree of truth belonging to the present stage in the development of human society. To suppose some unchanging religious truth, some definitive interpretation of reality, is to fall into ideology, because to do so is to deny concrete history with its persisting alienations and to escape into abstraction. It is equivalently to proclaim that reconciliation has been achieved in theory and thus nullify the imperative to change the world and achieve reconciliation in practice.

But if the religious interpretation of reality is, like all forms of knowledge, a social enterprise, historically mediated by social practice, neither faith nor theology can be considered on its own apart from the development of society in its total reality. A religious tradition cannot be studied apart from the social group that carries it. Particular social groups have to be considered in the context of society as a whole. Thus the history of faith with its interpretation and the history of society with its interpretation merge into one, and so do the study of religion and the study of society. Theology in the critical tradition cannot confine itself to religious data and evade the task of offering a general theory of society and history.

Human history is in large part a history of unmeaning and untruth, a story of domination and repression. Faith cannot

claim that it has remained pure and undefiled without denying its own social basis. For that reason faith, together with
theology, cannot be a genuine protest against domination and
injustice unless it acknowledges that it itself and its own past
history are the products of unfree society and therefore subject
to criticism and revolutionary transformation. Critical theology is ineluctably the critique of religion and of theology as
instances of domination.

However, unlike Marx, critical theology sees the critique of
religion as belonging to the dynamic of religion itself. This
brings me to the second line of reflection upon the thought of
Marx, namely concerning the dynamic behind critique. Marx
would seem to have identified that dynamic with science.

To what sources of experience does an emancipatory critique appeal? How do we recognize that we are unfree? What
leads us to struggle against domination, against untruth,
against alienation? How does our imperfect humanity anticipate its emancipated perfection as a possible ideal, not an illusion? Religious faith as a thrust towards plenitude and totality,
as a pursuit of transcendent truth and value may surely be
counted among the sources of emancipatory experience, and
as such self-criticism against its own imperfect and corrupt
manifestations is built into it.

The attitude of Marx to such an approach may be indirectly
established by his attitude to utopian socialism. A polemic
against utopian socialism was carried on by Marx and Engels.
'Utopian socialism was defined by them as the attempt to base
the construction of a socialist society on some kind of ideal
extracted from traditional religion, philosophical idealism, or
the poetical imagination. Scientific socialism, on the contrary,
would derive a concrete socialist society out of a scientific
analysis of concrete, actually existing social conditions' (Comstock, 1976: 328). The attitude of Marx emerges clearly in a dra-
matic confrontation between himself and Weitling, the
religious socialist, on 30 March 1846. Frostin reproduces
Annenkov's report in an appendix (1978: 186–8), but I will
draw upon the account of the incident and translation of
Annenkov in Padover's biography of Marx (1978: 226–33).
Marx turned to Weitling and asked:

Tell us, Weitling, you who have made so much noise in Germany with your communist preachings, you who have won over so many workers that they thereby lost their work and their bread, on what grounds do you justify your social-revolutionary activities, and on what do you expect to base them in the future?

Weitling protested that it was not his aim to create new economic theories, but Marx replied:

It is simply a fraud to arouse the people without providing them with firm, carefully thought out principles for their actions. The arousing of fantastic hopes, of the kind just heard here, would only end in the downfall of the suffering people, and not in their salvation. In Germany, to appeal to the workers without a strict scientific idea and without a positive doctrine, is like an empty and conscienceless game of propaganda, which on the one hand presupposes an inspired prophet and on the other, only donkeys listening to him with open mouth.

Angrily, Weitling recalled how he had brought together hundreds of men in the name of justice, solidarity and brotherly love and referred contemptuously to theories remote from the suffering world and the oppressions of the people. Marx flew into a great rage, and pounding his fist on the table he shouted: 'Ignorance has never yet helped anybody!'

It is not to my purpose to side with Weitling against Marx or to deny the emptiness of much religious preaching and moral exhortation, divorced as it is from an accurate and thorough analysis of the concrete situation. But is not the ambition of Marx to substitute science for utopian ideals an indication of his latent positivism? The latent positivism of Marx has been admitted and documented by the Frankfurt School. That raises the question for the next chapter whether the Frankfurt School has modified the Marxist critique of religion.

6

The language of religion and the language of politics

Max Horkheimer, looking back towards the end of his life at what he and Adorno had written in the *Dialectic of Enlightenment*, said in a passage I quoted in the first chapter: 'a politics which, even when highly unreflected, does not preserve a theological moment in itself is, no matter how skilful, in the last analysis, mere business' (1975: 60). There is, then, a theological moment in politics; a level at which talk about politics becomes theological talk. Political theology is not an heroic and, as some would say, forlorn effort to make theology politically relevant, but the articulation of the religious moment immanent in any politics that is not mere horse-trading.

When does politics become religion or, perhaps more concretely, when does political language become religious language? In a study of the distinctive character of religious language, Paul Ricoeur says that 'the properly religious moment of all discourse, including political discourse, is the "still more" that it insinuates everywhere, intensifying every project in the same manner, including the political project' (1975: 126). For him what constitutes language as religious is not its being a particular form of discourse, such as metaphor or parable or proclamation or proverb. Religious language is of many kinds, and no form of discourse is of itself religious. Language is religious by a modification, a transgression as it were, of the accepted functioning of its forms, so that they become limit-expressions, pointing beyond their immediate meaning towards the transcendent or Wholly Other. A form of discourse is made to function religiously by an intensification, the introduction of an element of extravagance, a going to the limit, which turns it, in Ian Ramsey's phrase, into an

133

'odd language' (1957). To become religious, ordinary language of diverse forms is disoriented, so that it then calls for reorientation on the level of higher meaning. It is in that way that political language can function religiously. Ricoeur writes:

> political discourse therefore is no less oriented, disoriented, and re-oriented than any other form of discourse; and the specific way in which it is disoriented and reoriented is that it becomes the place for the insertion of an impossible demand, a demand that we can validly interpret in utopian terms, meaning by this a quest that cannot be exhausted by any program of action (1975: 126–7).

Thus, when political language makes an 'impossible demand' in relation to human liberation and the reconciliation of human beings with the universe and with themselves, it has become religious. For the positivists, namely those who confine reason to what is empirical, quantifiable and admitting of technical control, it has thereby become irrational. For Horkheimer, on the other hand, the exclusion of theology makes a moral politics impossible. From the scientific standpoint, hate, he argues, is not more evil than love; there is no socio-functional difference. The logic of science can produce no reason why a person should not hate if it is to his advantage to do so. Morality cannot in the last analysis be grounded on a worldly prudence; it has to refer to a Beyond and thus go back to a theology (1975: 60–1).

The neo-Marxist Horkheimer, founder of the Critical Theory, clearly does not agree with the early Marx that religion has no content of its own and is simply the illusory articulation of the divisions and contradictions of society in its secular basis. All the same, Horkheimer, together with the Frankfurt School as a whole, continues the critique of religion as this has developed in the West since the Enlightenment (Siebert, 1976 a, b/and c). Although Horkheimer and Adorno were painfully aware of the ambiguity of the Enlightenment and, particularly in their joint work, *Dialectic of Enlightenment*, showed how its striving to dominate nature has issued in the domination of man, they remained committed to the Enlightenment ideal of emancipation with its stress on autonomous reason and freedom, including its rejection of religion and of Christianity in particular. In a short but compact essay he wrote in 1935, which is reproduced in *Critical Theory: Selected Essays*, Horkheimer states flatly: 'Mankind loses religion as it moves through history' (1972: 131); and again: 'It is a vain hope that contemporary debates in the church would make religion once again the vital reality it was in the beginning. Good will, solidarity with wretchedness, and the struggle for a better world have now thrown off their religious garb' (*ibid.*, 130).

The age of religion is therefore past without recall. Nevertheless, it has left its mark behind. Horkheimer begins by stressing the protest character of religion:

The concept of God was for a long time the place where the idea was kept alive that there are other norms besides those to which nature and society give expression in their operation. Dissatisfaction with earthly destiny is the strongest motive for acceptance of a transcendental being. If justice resides with God, then it is not to be found in the same measure in the world. Religion is the record of the wishes, desires, and accusations of countless generations (*ibid.*, 129).

With the dissolution of religion, the more productive elements in the protest embodied in religion pass over into a practical struggle for more rational forms of social life. But what happens to the image of perfect justice or what may be called the excess or immoderation in religious belief and longing?

In the essay I have cited Horkheimer insists that perfect justice is an illusion and improbably, I think, suggests that it arose out of primitive exchange. 'The principle', he writes, 'that each one must have his share and that each one has the same basic right to happiness is a generalization of economically conditioned rules, their extension into the infinite' (*ibid.*, 130). All the same, while shattering the illusion of perfect justice, he wishes to retain the concept of the infinite precisely as an awareness of limits: 'In a really free mind the concept of infinity is preserved in an awareness of the finality of human life and of the inalterable aloneness of men, and it keeps society from indulging in thoughtless optimism, an inflation of its own knowledge into a new religion' (*ibid.*, 131).

'The inalterable aloneness of men' – here is struck the note of metaphysical and cultural pessimism that characterizes the older generation of the Frankfurt School. Horkheimer did not derive that from Marx, who, despite the vehemence of his negative criticism, is optimistic in his basic outlook. We need to remember that Horkheimer read Schopenhauer when he was eighteen, two years before he began to read Marx (1975: 15–17), and it is from Schopenhauer and Hegel, we may add, he derives his pessimism. There was also his experience as a German Jew and refugee from Nazism. Confronted with the horrors of the twentieth century, Horkheimer shared the conviction of those who found that the suffering and injustice beyond measure of this world now made it impossible to believe in an almighty and all-loving God.

What is basic for Horkheimer is the consciousness of our finitude and abandonment. This consciousness does not prove the existence of God, but it does produce the hope that there is a positive Absolute. We have no certitude about God, but the thought of God accompanies and confirms our sense of finitude. If we did have an absolute certitude that there was a God, our knowledge of our state of abandonment as human beings would have become a deception. But that cannot be so. That we are alone is too clear for denial.

Horkheimer links his agnosticism with Judaism, namely, with its hesitation to utter or write the word 'God' and with the prohibition, unique to itself among religions, against the making of images. Judaism, with its stress upon doing, upon keeping the prescriptions of the law, rather than upon beliefs, is also, he thinks, closer to Catholicism than to Protestantism. The concept of faith, he suggests, is largely a Protestant invention. The Protestants tried to find a middle way between superstition on the one hand and science on the other and came up with faith. Horkheimer remains Jewish in holding that the stress should be on doing rather than on believing. If that is so, is the question of God of any importance to him? He answers that it is both unimportant and important. Unimportant, because we cannot affirm anything about the existence or nature of God. Important, because behind all genuine human action there stands theology.

What Horkheimer is doing in that paradoxical way is putting forward an extreme form of negative theology. Theology for him is the consciousness that the world is appearance, that it is not the absolute truth, the ultimate. More concretely, theology is the hope that injustice does not have the last word, the longing that the murderer may not triumph over his victim (1975: 61–2).

To put it in another way, theology for him is the opposite of positivism. Horkheimer's appeal to the Absolute, his yearning for the Wholly Other, is the expression of his rejection of positivism and of his concern for the destructive social and ethical consequences of its present unchecked advance. For him positivism makes moral politics impossible by removing any cogent reason why human beings should love rather than hate, pursue freedom rather than domination. He invokes the Absolute to relativize the present social order, which, since the economic recovery after the Second World War, has been carried forward on a wave of positivism towards the cybernetic goal of a totally administered society.

But he remained pessimistic. Admittedly, he allowed the possibility that in the totally administered society of the future theology or the longing for the Absolute might persist. Since all material needs will be satisfied, men and women may become even more conscious of the fact of death, and out of the sense of finitude and mortality may come a new solidarity amongst them, which might weaken the grip of the total administration. But the final paragraph of his book on *Die Sehnsucht nach dem ganz Anderen* envisages the alternative possibility that in the totally administered society of the future theology would be given up and with it would disappear from the world everything that we call meaning. There will be much busy activity, but it will be meaningless and boring. Theology and philosophy will be regarded as belonging to the childhood of the race. Any speculation about the relation between the transcendent and the relative will be regarded as foolishness, and philosophy and theology will have come to an end (1975: 88–9). One may put alongside that gloomy prognosis, published by Horkheimer three years before his death, a report we have about his friend and co-worker, Adorno: 'Adorno's students observed in the eyes and gestures of their teacher an expression of deep sadness, anxiety and horror concerning the senescence process of Western civilization during the last months before his death in 1969' (Siebert, 1974: 68).

In sum, Horkheimer denied that we had any certain

knowledge of the existence and nature of God; indeed, he rejected the traditional concept of an all-powerful and all-loving God as untenable in the light of human suffering. He also regarded the image of perfect justice or of a fully reconciled society as an illusion. Nevertheless, for him, as he wrote: 'What distinguishes the progressive type of man from the retrogressive is not the refusal of the idea but the understanding of the limits set to its fulfillment' (1972: 130). The thought or, as he also says, the hope of the Absolute, the Wholly Other, the Infinite, keeps us aware of our finitude and aloneness, relativizes our society and makes a moral politics and genuine solidarity possible.

There is a Stoic dignity in the melancholic attitude I have sketched. But surely the standpoint is an unstable one. Behind any thought that is not illusion, behind every hope that is not wishful thinking, there must be some affirmation of reality. Certainly, any theology that demands to be taken seriously today will be of a predominantly negative kind, but a negative theology that refuses any affirmation concerning the reality of the Absolute destroys its own basis. If God is totally unknown or wholly incomprehensible, there is no reason to connect him with hope rather than with despair. It is also difficult to see how hope without an affirmation of a real alternative to injustice can check the triumphant march of positivism – that it cannot is shown by Horkheimer's final despair.

A similar response may be made to the even more negative position of Adorno, whose 'negative dialectics' is the refusal of any positive position. 'Dialectics', he writes, 'is the consistent sense of nonidentity. It does not begin by taking a standpoint. My thought is driven to it by its own inevitable insufficiency, by my guilt of what I am thinking' (1973: 5). But Adorno's negative dialectics is intended as a critique of society and as such it has a strongly moral character. The refusal to affirm explicitly the moral position that is its ground leaves it unstable and inconsistent in its functioning.

Habermas, the younger representative of the Frankfurt School (he was born in 1929), did not remain content with the unsystematic reflections of his elders. His effort has been to make criticism scientific and, in doing so, to elaborate a comprehensive and systematic theory of society. It is fairly safe to surmise that he is antipathetic to the unmistakably religious longings of the later Horkheimer. 'The hope', wrote Horkheimer, 'that earthly horror does not possess the last word is, to be sure, a non-scientific wish' (Jay, 1973: xii). But Habermas sets out to see how far emancipatory hopes can be rationally grounded in a science of communication. As for the rest, we must simply live without consolation.

For Habermas the traditional world-views as represented by the religions have been dismantled beyond any prospect of restoration. Two chief factors, one socio-structural, the other cognitive, account for their dissolution (1976a: 79).

First, a steady rationalization has brought area after area of life previously regulated by tradition under the control of rational techniques. The result is a discrepancy between religion with its traditions and the socio-structural forces behind the economic and administrative systems of capitalist society. Habermas himself is critical of the onesidedness of this rationalizing process. It has been carried out and interpreted exclusively in terms of a means–end or purposive rationality, systematizing instrumental action with its technical rules and strategic action with its rules of choice, but overlooking the distinctive character of communicative action with its norms. He does not however envisage any renewal of the normative function of religion with its conventional mode of action, bound to tradition, but proposes instead a distinctive rationalization of normative action through the free and equal participation of all concerned in a process of rational will-formation.

Second, an incompatibility has grown up between religious tradition and the cognitive attitudes flowing from science. This cognitive dissonance between the religious and scientific outlooks has become widespread in a positivistic common sense. Religion as a world-view has lost its place because modern culture no longer looks for a world-view in the sense of an interpretation of the world, nature and history as a whole. World-views have been replaced by transitory syntheses of scientific information or by imaginative inventions (1976a: 80). The relation between religion and philosophy has changed. Philosophy has given up its claim to provide an ultimate foundation, and hence it is no longer in a position, as it was, to take up the religious concept of the one God into a metaphysics of the One or the Absolute. Post-metaphysical thought no longer disputes individual theological assertions, but declares the meaninglessness of all theological statements (1971a: 27). This, I may note, does scant justice to the philosophical discussions on religious language.

Habermas suggests that science may to a limited extent take the place of the dissolved world-views. He writes:

it has in no way been determined that the philosophical impulse to conceive of a demythologized unity of the world cannot also be retained through scientific argumentation. Science can certainly not take over the functions of world-views. But general theories (whether of social development or of nature) contradict consistent scientific thought less than its positivistic self-misunderstanding. Like the irrecoverably criticized world-views, such theoretical strategies also hold the promise of meaning: the overcoming of contingencies. But, at the same time, they aim at methodically removing from this promise the ambivalence between truth claim and a merely illusory fulfillment. We can no longer avert recognizable contingencies by producing a rationalizing illusion (1976a: 121).

The last sentence indirectly indicates that Habermas shares the atheistic conviction of Horkheimer and Adorno concerning the metaphysical aloneness or abandonment of human beings, though he does so without their pathos and without Horkheimer's hopeful yearning for the Wholly Other. His own statement is coldly emphatic:

Considering the risks to individual life that exist, a theory that could interpret away the facticities of loneliness and guilt, sickness and death is, to be sure, not even *conceivable*. Contingencies that are irremovably attached to the bodily and moral constitution of the individual can be raised to consciousness only *as* contingency. We must, in principle, live disconsolately with them (*ibid.*, 120 – Habermas's italics).

Habermas, however, does not go along with the early Marx in holding that religion is simply nothing. Instead, he agrees with Bloch that religion as the negation of the negation of humanity is full of encoded experiences. He writes:

Within the ideological shell Bloch discovers the Utopian core, within the as yet false consciousness the true consciousness. Certainly, the transparency of a better world is refracted by hidden interests, even in those aspects which point beyond the existing state; but still, the hopes which it awakens, the longings which it satisfies, contain energies that at the same time, once instructed about themselves, become critical impulses (1974a: 239).

Habermas shows concern that with the atheism of the masses – religion today, he thinks, has ceased to be even a personal matter – the utopian contents of tradition are also threatened (1976a: 80). He regards religious systems of interpretation as irretrievably obsolete. His own effort is to detach the rational core of the utopian content of religion and incorporate it into his practical philosophy of communication. The religious utopia of a liberated and reconciled community thus becomes the secular ideal of unconstrained communication among equal participants in a community free from domination.

I want to leave further consideration of Habermas's theory of religion until the next chapter, because he interprets the history of religion in relation to the problem of social identity, which is part of the subject-matter I am going to treat there. In general, here, I may remark that Habermas sees the history of religion as encompassing various past stages in the development of communicative practice in society and the related constitution of different forms of ego and group identity. But he regards the previously operative systems of religious interpretation and orientation as obsolete, so that the end of the development manifested in the history of the religion is the communicative competence of free and equal subjects to engage in a reciprocal process of will-formation, so as to reach agreement concerning norms and courses of action. Religion, therefore, as an interpretative system is superseded by a practical philosophy of communicative practice and the normative function of religion is replaced by an explicitly self-conscious process of communication, free from domination.

The question put to Habermas by the theologian, Peukert, is whether there are dimensions in the structure of communicative action that may lead us back to a reconsideration of the Christian tradition and perhaps also to the contribution of other religious traditions (1976: 229). This question is best approached by considering the problem of human solidarity as it was raised by some remarks of Walter Benjamin, another member of the Frankfurt School.

In an exchange with Horkheimer in 1937 (Peukert, 1976: 278–9), Benjamin declared that the work of the past is not finished and closed off; it cannot be reified and possessed like a piece of property. Horkheimer disagreed. The past is finished. Past injustice has happened and is done with. The slain are truly slain. That reaction corresponds to a steady conviction of Horkheimer, which he expressed on a number of occasions around this time. 'Past injustice', he wrote, 'will never be made up; the suffering of past generations receives no compensation' (1972: 26). The image of perfect justice he declared an illusion: 'For, even if a better society develops and eliminates the present disorder, there will be no compensation for the wretchedness of past ages and no end to the distress in nature' (*ibid.*, 130). Again:

What has happened to past generations, no future can mend. They will never be called up to be rewarded in eternity. Nature and society have left their evil imprint on them and the idea of a Last Judgment, reflective though it may be of the infinite longing of the repressed and the dying, is but a residue of primitive thought which fails to understand the insignificant role man has been playing in natural history and which falsely humanizes the universe.[17]

Horkheimer did insist that wishes for eternity and particularly for the coming of universal justice and goodness were something materialistic thinkers had in common with religious thinkers. It marked off both groups from the positivists with their obtuse indifference. But while the religious thinker believes in a fulfilment to these wishes, the materialist thinker is penetrated with a sense of the limitless abandonment of men, in which for him lies the only true answer to that impossible hope (1968: I, 372).

It was not surprising, therefore, that Horkheimer, when confronted with Benjamin's assertion that history was unfinished and open, replied: 'In the last analysis your statement is theological' (Peukert, 1976: 279). Benjamin did not at that time take up the challenge of Horkheimer, but he had already written in an unpublished piece:

Remembrance can make of the unfinished (i.e. happiness) something that is finished and, conversely, it can make the finished (i.e. past suffering) into something that is unfinished. This is theology.

Yet in remembering we gain the knowledge that we must not try to understand history in fundamentally a-theological terms, just as we would not want to write history in straightforwardly theological terms (quoted in Lenhardt, 1975: 141–2).

It is likely enough that the exchange with Horkheimer stimulated the process of thought that resulted a few years later in Benjamin's 'Theses on the idea of history', written in 1940 and published posthumously in 1950. In these fascinating and enigmatic reflections, Benjamin is striving after a conception of history that will not renounce a basic solidarity with the past generations of the oppressed and slain, but will preserve that solidarity and thus grasp history as the history of suffering (*Leidensgeschichte*).

It is difficult without lengthy quotation to give a true impression of either the content or the tone of that unusual document. It is available in *Illuminations*, the English selection of Benjamin's writings, edited by Hannah Arendt. Here are some scattered sentences:

The past carries with it a temporal index by which it is referred to redemption. There is a secret agreement between past generations and the present one. Our coming was expected on earth . . . . To be sure, only a redeemed mankind receives the fullness of its past – which is to say, only for a redeemed mankind has its past become citable in all its moments . . . . In every era the attempt must be made anew to wrest tradition away from a conformism that is about to overpower it. The Messiah comes not only as the redeemer, he comes as the subduer of Antichrist. Only that historian will have the gift of fanning the spark of hope in the past who is firmly convinced that *even the dead* will not be safe from the enemy if he wins . . . . Not man or men but the struggling, oppressed class itself is the depository of historical knowledge. In Marx it appears as the last enslaved class, as the avenger that completes the task of liberation in the name of generations of the downtrodden . . . . Social Democracy thought fit to assign to the working class the role of the redeemer of future generations, in this way cutting the sinews of its strength. This training made the working class forget both its hatred and its spirit of sacrifice, for both are nourished by the image of enslaved ancestors rather than that of liberated grandchildren . . . . History is the subject of a structure whose site is not homogeneous, empty time, but time filled by the presence of the new (*Jetztzeit*) (1973: 256–63 – Benjamin's italics).

The clash between Horkheimer and Benjamin and the further reflections of Benjamin on history bring us up against what has been called the aporia of redemptive solidarity or, less theologically, the solidarity of emancipated mankind. In an article of remarkable originality, 'Anamnestic solidarity: the proletariat and its *Manes*', Christian Lenhardt sets up a kind of thought-experiment. Let G_1 stand for the generation of enslaved predecessors, G_2 for the generation of enslaved contemporaries, who, according to Marx, will emancipate themselves, and G_3 for the generation of emancipated successors. Are we to see the solidarity of a liberated mankind simply in terms of harmony amongst the members of G_3? 'This', says Lenhardt, 'would reduce the exploited predecessors (G_1) and those who struggle for the revolutionary cause (G_2) to the status of nonentities or dead wood in the evolution of mankind, primitive stages which had to be overcome, and whose existence had better be forgotten' (1975: 135–6). He then asks: 'Is Marxism really the theory and practice of emancipation from remembrance? Is it a synonym for a pervasive world-historical amnesia?' (*ibid.*, 136). But G_3, the emancipated generation, is in a peculiar difficulty in regard to its debt to the preceding generations. G_2, the emancipating generation, has a debt to G_1, the enslaved generation, in so far as the latter provided, however blindly and unknowingly, the historical opportunity for the overthrow of unfreedom, but it pays off that debt by the self-sacrifice of its emancipatory struggle. But how does G_3 pay off its debts? Lenhardt continues:

If a redemptive attitude is part and parcel of the ideal of emancipated mankind, is it not rather an unenviable destiny to belong to the successor generation (G_3), for what can it do, practically and existentially, to equalize the burden of injustice borne by its predecessors (G_1 and G_2)? Must it not passively accept the gifts of the dead, as gods were said to accept the hecatombs of those who believed in them? If that were the point of the revolution, its alleged humanization would be tantamount to the deification of man: a perversion of the notion of species being (*ibid.*, 137–8).

In other words, the liberated generation cannot be ingenuous in its appropriation of the world. 'The evils of prehistory may have been overcome', Lenhardt argues, 'but they will linger on the collective *anamnesis* of liberated mankind. They must so linger, or else the achievement of true solidarity is just another form of one-dimensional experience where enjoyment of the Thing and the Other is as unreflective as it is under conditions of late-capitalist affluence' (*ibid.*, 138 – Lenhardt's italics). In brief, there must be what Lenhardt calls anamnestic solidarity – a solidarity in remembrance. The liberated generation 'to live nobly must *learn* that it owes everything and possesses nothing' (*ibid.*, 139 – Lenhardt's italics). He concludes:

By recognizing that the victorious proletarian contemporaries would be *de facto* heirs of legions of exploited slaves and workers of the past, Marx illuminates in a flash the essence of anamnestic solidarity. The unity of repressed mankind is the solidarity of the living with the dead. Marx calls for an understanding of class in terms of the continuity of exploitation across the ages. If the impending revolution goes forth without being informed by this larger historical solidarity with the dead, then it will only wipe out one injustice by replacing it with another. The historical meaning of such a spurious revolution would be that of a second, posthumous expropriation of those who spent their lives in slavery. A revolutionary working-class which takes for granted that its predecessors sacrificed themselves for its own well-being is a working-class without heart (*ibid.*, 151).

Lenhardt, a political scientist, does not do more than insist upon remembrance, which he relates to the religious practice of ancestor-worship. Peukert, a theologian, goes much further and sees the paradox of anamnestic solidarity as uncovering the limits of a theory of communicative action when used, as in Habermas, normatively as the rational grounding of emancipatory values, but without any theological dimension.

At the heart of intersubjective communication we confront a boundary experience, namely the annihilation of the innocent other. I mean, a man or woman to whom we have reached out in solidarity, to whose sharing with us in community we owe our own possibilities for life and growth, is without any fault removed and reduced to nothingness by death. No adequate theory of communicative action can evade the question of human solidarity with the partners in community who, without any proportionate or just reason, are destroyed, but who still are remembered. Habermas, in a passage I have already quoted, puts death among the contingencies 'irremovably attached to the bodily and moral constitution of the individual' and declares inconceivable any theory that could interpret such contingencies away (1976a: 120). He overlooks that death affects, not just the constitution of the individual, but the structure of communicative action. Let us grant that to seek a theory that, as he puts it, would interpret death away is clearly inadmissible. But, surely, it is equally inadmissible to construct a theory of communicative action that evades the aporia created by death.

The boundary experience as I have described it is richly significant, because it includes other experiences within itself that likewise leave us in a distressful bafflement. There is the experience that a man or woman can give to or take away from another his or her possibilities for life or growth. There are the contingencies of pain and sickness, sometimes so destructive of community, though remaining short of death. Then there is the general fact of death itself, even when it is no longer seen as striking down the just and innocent. The other with whom we communicate or try to communicate is irrevocably removed from us. The possibility of mutual presence in communicative action is destroyed. From this standpoint Peukert urges a reconsideration of the Judaeo-Christian tradition, arguing that its basic apprehension of the reality of God is related to the experience of the annihilation of the innocent other. He outlines a proposal for a new fundamental theology. As a basis for theology, this would elaborate a theory, first, of communicative action, taken truly universally and including therefore a solidarity with the dead, and, second, of the reality of God as disclosed and experienced in that action (1976: 315–23). To express his contention in another way, it is that a theory of communicative action becomes theology when it includes – as it must do if it is to be truly comprehensive – the experience of God, an experience we find to be implicit in human interaction.

Here is a brief sketch of Peukert's line of argument.

What can we do when confronted with the death of the partner or partners in communication, to interaction with whom we perhaps owe our personal identity or, at least, some of the possibilities we have for living? We can try to erase any dead person, however previously significant, from our memory. But any such attempt is simply a refusal to accept reality and, like all similar attempts, undermines the whole of our knowledge. Or, the experience of the inevitable annihilation of all partners in any human solidarity of action can provoke the cynical conclusion that everyone should simply act for himself or herself alone, making optimal use of the selfish possibilities offered. But this would precisely mean the destruction of communicative action as a distinctive form of human action and the reduction of all human action to instrumental or strategic action, namely to action oriented either to technical success or to success in defeating the game-plan of others seen as opponents and in winning one's own. It would be the end of human community, built as this is upon actions oriented to mutual understanding and agreement, not to individual or group success. Human community is likewise destroyed if, more naively and resignedly, one sees human beings as finite creatures of nature, locked in a struggle with one another for existence, and thus accepts for them a falling back below the evolutionary threshold of communicative action and its norms.

None of those possible ways of dealing with the death of our partners in human communication is acceptable. If we are not to reject the fundamental structure of human communication or fall into self-contradiction, we have to preserve the memory of all the victims of history and retain an unconditional, universal solidarity with them in concrete action. That means that the concrete practice of a person truly involved in communicative action, for whom therefore the unconditional acknowledgement of the other person is the condition of possibility for his own identity and growth, implies a refusal in fact to accept the annihilation of the other person. Peukert then appeals to the Judaeo-Christian tradition and with it affirms that in communicative action, understood as a solidarity in time among persons moving towards death, there is an anticipatory grasp of a reality that can and does save the other whom we meet in solidarity. It may be noted that he denies the usual assumption that the death of the other is secondary in respect to the anticipation of one's own death. The thought of one's own death may confront us, in Heidegger's phrase, with the possibility of the impossibility of existence. But it is our solidarity with the other in death that discloses the saving reality towards which death points. To resume: the concrete practice of those engaged in genuinely communicative action implies the assertion of a reality that saves from death. The reality, disclosed in communicative action as a saving reality and implicitly asserted on the level of practice by that action, is the reality we name God. The situation of communicative action thus becomes an originating source, making possible talk about God.

What Peukert has done is to adopt the procedure of Habermas and carry it forward into a theology. Habermas makes an analysis of communicative action the point of departure for a critical theory of society. He shows how communicative action presupposes the mutual recognition of validity claims, which require justification in discourse as a further level of communication. Discourse as communication however rests upon a normative foundation, implying the acceptance of the emancipatory values of truth, freedom and justice. The analysis of communication, therefore, provides us with a rational grounding of those values, in so far as it shows that their assertion is implicit in every instance of communicative action. Communicative action, he maintains, is an irreducible and indispensable form of human action. Peukert picks up the argument at this point and urges that communicative action confronts us with the boundary experience of the death of the innocent partner. Death destroys the solidarity created by communicative action, on which we depend for our identity and growth. To affirm communicative action as an irreducible and indispensable element of human existence without evading the fact of death or falling into self-contradiction is to affirm the presence of a reality that saves from death and thus discloses itself in human solidarity. In brief, it is to affirm God as the Judaeo-Christian tradition presents him.

Fundamental theology as Peukert proposes it would take the form of a theological theory of communicative action, developed in an interdisciplinary fashion in relation with linguistics, communication theory, social psychology and the sociological theory of action. It would extend outwards from a theory of communicative action to include a theory of the subject, a theory of society and a theory of history. Peukert's proposal illustrates what I said in chapter 3 about critical theology as a comprehensive theory of society and history. I added that a theological critical theory of that kind would function as an explanatory component in a theological critique of ideology, namely a critique from a theological standpoint of the ideological elements in religious tradition and practice, those elements that have made religion a form of domination. Peukert's proposal on its part emphasizes the positive function of critical theory in uncovering the foundation for a purified religion and theology.

Peukert, I have noted, appeals in his argument to the Judaeo-Christian tradition. It is indeed his conviction that talk of freedom is not possible, unless one turns back in remembrance to freedom as historically experienced and realized (1976: 313). Hence he readily admits that the analysis he has given of communicative action and of the experiences it provokes would scarcely have been thinkable apart from the tradition of the Old Testament and the coming of Jesus of Nazareth.

There he is taking up what Metz says about remembrance in relation to emancipation and the whole complex of values we designate briefly as freedom. Metz has analysed remembrance as a basic philosophical concept (1973b). He has put forward the theological thesis of the *memoria Christi*, the remembrance of the passion, death and resurrection of Christ as a dangerous and liberating memory (1970b). It is dangerous, because it breaks into our everyday world, puts the present in question and challenges the established powers. On this point Metz quotes repeatedly in his writings this passage from Marcuse's *One-dimensional Man*:

Remembrance of the past can allow dangerous perceptions to dawn upon us. The social establishment seems to fear the subversive content of such recollections. Remembrance is a way of detaching oneself from the given situation, a kind of 'intervention', which for an instant interrupts the omnipotence of the given situation. Rememberance recalls past misery as well as past hope (1964: 98; quoted by Metz 1969a: 40; 1969b: 287; 1970b: 15; 1972a: 126; 1973b: 392; 1977a: 171).

More generally, Metz argues that freedom today has become an arbitrary concept. It is incorporated into any and every system. The only way to give such a fluid concept some consistency is to connect it with a tradition having an interest in freedom. Concern with freedom and the appropriating remembrance of a tradition are no longer opposed. Indeed an analysis of our present culture shows that tradition has become the condition for giving a clear, meaningful content to the concept of freedom. The post-historical forms of knowledge, which characterize the present stage of Western culture, are gradually eliminating any interest in freedom. Our society has, as it were, less and less memory; it is under the anonymous dictatorship of a one-dimensional now. Consequently, the present situation differs from that of the Enlightenment, when freedom was opposed to authority, reason to tradition and history to institutions. Concern with freedom now remains living only within the framework provided by those traditions from which it originally emerged (Metz, Moltmann, Oelmüller, 1970: 38).

It is in that context that Metz defines faith as remembrance. 'Christian faith', he writes, 'is therefore understood here as that attitude according to which men remember promises that have been made and hopes that have been lived in the light of those promises and bind themselves to those memories in a way that determines their life' (Peukert, ed., 1969: 286). Metz's concept may be related to the statement of Paul Ricoeur that faith is self-understanding in the face of a text. Faith is a mediated experience, dependent upon entry through interpretive understanding into a world maintained by a tradition and handed on in the texts of that tradition. Ricoeur writes:

For a hermeneutical philosophy, faith never appears as an immediate experience, but always as mediated by a certain language which articulates it. For my part I should link the concept of faith to that of *self-understanding* in the face of the text. Faith is the attitude of one who accepts being interpreted at the same time that he interprets the world of the text. Such is the hermeneutical constitution of the biblical faith (1974: 84 – Ricoeur's italics).

Whatever may be the hermeneutical moment in all our knowledge – and I have suggested in chapter 4 that it is always present and much larger than Habermas, for example, admits – there is little doubt that personal faith as a basic insight or a fundamental orientation to reality is mediated through the interpretation of a tradition. Faith comes to us as the personal appropriation of the collective remembrance of a community, a remembrance that has accumulated a long historical experience, together with many attempts at its expression.

The close relationship between faith and tradition rests upon the historical and cumulative mode of the human apprehension of values and grasp of spiritual reality. Theologically interpreted, the relationship is also grounded in faith's being a response to a divine initiative. This, though it penetrates the inward centre of the individual, is present primarily in the concrete practice of human history. The disclosure of God as saving reality is to be placed chiefly in human history seen as a history of suffering and of struggle for liberation. The experience of the presence of God as saving reality in the death of those with whom we are unconditionally joined in communicative action would remain a weak and inarticulate sentiment, were it not strengthened and given expression in the repeatedly renewed reading and interpretation of the stories of the Old and New Testaments. Our questions themselves, not just the answers we seek, are prompted and articulated by tradition.

When he appeals to the Judaeo-Christian tradition, Peukert also declares that story or narrative is the primordial way in which the experiences provoked by the boundary situations become present and are mediated (1976: 313). Here, again, he is picking up the thought of Metz, who more recently has stressed the theological importance of narrative.

Metz presents his ideas succinctly in the article. 'A short apology of narrative' (1973c – reproduced in a revised form in 1977a: 181–94). He does so seemingly with no knowledge of the considerable literature produced in the last decade in North America on the theology of story. Instead, his reflections originate from an essay of Walter Benjamin, 'The storyteller' (1973: 83–109). Benjamin describes the function of the story as the exchange of experiences and notes its gradual disappearance from our culture. 'Experience', he writes, 'which is passed on from mouth to mouth is the source from which all storytellers have drawn .... The storyteller takes what he tells from experience – his own or that reported by others. And he in turn makes it the experience of those who are listening to his tale' (*ibid.*, 84, 87). But the communicability of experience is decreasing, and the new form of communication is information, with its appeal to prompt verifiability (*ibid.*, 88–9). 'It is as if something that seemed inalienable to us, the securest among our possessions, were taken from us: the ability to exchange experiences' (*ibid.*, 83). Using Benjamin's remarks as a starting-point, Metz argues that theology 'is above all concerned with direct experiences expressed in narrative language' (1973c: 85). Narrative is not just a useful aid in teaching, but a mode of expression fundamental to faith and theology, because only through narrative can history and salvation be brought into relationship. Metz refers to the new marginal groups, such as the Jesus People, and sees them as reminding us that 'Christians do not primarily form an argumentative and reasoning community, but a story-telling community and that the exchange of experiences of faith, like that of any "new" experience, takes a narrative form' (*ibid.*, 88). Peukert on his part points to the newness or innovative character of the relevant experience as the reason why narrative remains the prime form of their expression. 'Newness' here, I take it, is not in contradiction to remembrance and the historical or traditional character of the experience. Religious experience is always new in as much as it is a transcending of the existing world and an opening of men and women to new possibilities of existence. Every existing world is moving towards death, and religious experience is the overcoming of death. But more of that in a moment.

Story or narrative – I am using the two terms synonymously [18] – is the fundamental form of religious language, because it is the fundamental mode of expression for human experience in general. Storytelling is the original and indispensable way we articulate our understanding of the world and the self. Theories or rational argumentation can never abrogate primal narrative consciousness. But for that very reason, storytelling is not exclusively religious; nor is religious language to be identified exclusively with sacred stories, for there are other forms.

Storytelling is not exclusively religious. I am speaking of storytelling, not as entertainment, but as the basic articulation of individual and group experience. As such, it is the primordial form of political as well as of religious language. When politics is understood with Aristotle as concerned with the good and just life, not merely with efficient administration, with ends therefore not simply with means, its language cannot be exclusively nor chiefly the theoretical language of science and the technical language of the administrator, but includes those forms of language appropriate to the articulation of ends and to communicative action among free persons seeking agreement. Among such forms of language, story or narrative is fundamental.

The expulsion of religion from politics and the over-hasty conclusion that all socially constitutive stories or myths were essentially religious allowed politics to be invaded by a technological consciousness, which saw justice as nothing but efficient reorganization of the State and a rational, impersonally impartial administration. What human beings are for or what constitutes a good human existence or what it is about human beings that makes them worthy of unconditional respect are all questions now considered beyond politics. We are apparently headed for the totally administered society, run according to the latest empirical theories and technical know-how. To avoid this requires a recognition that human consciousness is a consciousness entwined in stories, so that this consciousness in stories is, as Metz puts it, 'the only alternative to a world of total manipulation and absence of freedom' (1973c: 96).

Perhaps a return to a richer, more humane conception of politics and a consequent rewidening of the range of political language must come from an acknowledgement of the essentially religious dimension of communicative action. Politics, I repeat, is an affair of communicative action; the limitation of politics to instrumental or technical action is its death. But communicative action, as we have seen, runs up against aporias, which religious faith alone can meet. Politics and religion are distinct, but they depend upon each other for their healthy functioning. If political action mediates religious faith, religious faith in its turn mediates a truly humane politics. The continuity may be expressed in this image from Walter Benjamin:

> All great storytellers have in common the freedom with which they
> move up and down the rungs of their experience as on a ladder. A
> ladder extending downward to the interior of the earth and disap-
> pearing into the clouds is the image for a collective experience to
> which even the deepest shock of every individual experience, death,
> constitutes no impediment or barrier (1973: 103).

To put it this way: Can a society achieve a humane politics
without confronting the fact of death? Can it face death, with
its destruction of the very meaning of communicative, that is,
political action, without a religious interpretation?

If storytelling is not exclusively religious, religious language
on its part does not consist solely in storytelling. Religious
language includes narrative, such as myths and parables, but
also proverbs, lyrics, prayers, law-texts on the first-order level
and commentaries and theories on the second-order level of
theological language. Language as religious cannot be identified with any single type of expression or form of discourse.
What makes it religious is its pointing to mystery. Since
mystery cannot be directly apprehended or expressed, religious language is symbolic in the sense of having a double
intentionality, a double level of sense and reference. There is
the immediate meaning the language – the words, sentences,
literary forms – bears when interpreted within the context of
the everyday world. This immediate meaning is shattered by
some device or other; it is rendered inoperative, implausible,
inconsequential, so that the expression is either dismissed as
nonsense or reinterpreted as having a deeper meaning, disclosing mystery. The immediate sense and reference, though
eclipsed, are not entirely destroyed. They remain to serve in
various degrees as symbolic elements, helping indirectly to
express the directly inexpressible mystery. Various procedures are used to move language from its immediate to a religious sense and reference. Ricoeur has examined the
function of extravagance and intensification in parables and
proverbs from the first-order level (1975: 107–22), and Ian
Ramsey has spoken of 'qualifiers' on the level of theological
discourse (1957).

I should like to go outside biblical language to illustrate the
functioning of religious language by citing the example of the
fiction of Flannery O'Connor. Her writing has an undoubted

154

religious dimension, which has led one recent critic to speak of her stories as parables (May, 1976). She herself in her talks and essays keeps coming back to a distinction between manners and mystery, so that the editors of the posthumous collection of her occasional writings chose for them the title, *Mystery and Manners*. 'Manners' corresponds to what I have called the immediate meaning. For the fiction writer it is the level of concrete detail concerning the characters, their conventions and motivations, the context of their lives. But all that became for O'Connor a vehicle for a movement towards mystery:

The serious fiction writer will think that any story that can be entirely explained by the adequate motivation of the characters or by a believable imitation of a way of life or by a proper theology, will not be a large enough story for him to occupy himself with. This is not to say that he doesn't have to be concerned with adequate motivation or accurate reference or a right theology; he does; but he has to be concerned with them only because the meaning of his story does not begin except at a depth where these things have been exhausted. The fiction writer presents mystery through manners, grace through nature, but when he finishes, there always has to be left over that sense of mystery which cannot be accounted for by any human formula (1969: 153).

If one now asks what device or procedure O'Connor used to twist language from its immediate meaning towards mystery, then the answer lies in her use of the grotesque. The element of the grotesque in her fiction has often been noted and she herself comments upon it in her talks and essays. I think it serves a similar function to the extravagance that characterizes the Gospel parables and invites us to give those otherwise simple stories of everyday life an eschatological meaning.

Religious language points to mystery; it thus refers to God. But that, clearly, does not exhaust its content. In referring to God, it is also speaking to us about ourselves, about our lives, about the world. What, then, in general terms does it say about these matters? In other words, what distinguishes the religious mode of speech concerning the self, other people, the world, from other kinds of talk on the same topics? It is, I suggest, that religious language is an ever-renewed re-description of human experience and worldly reality according to unexpected and unformulable possibilities.

Let me explain:

First, religious language is concerned with common human experience and worldly reality. We must not allow its vertical dimension or reference to God to eliminate the horizontal dimension, which includes the whole of human existence.

Second, it constantly redescribes human experience and worldly reality, because no actual state of affairs corresponds to the hope that animates the religious vision. Religious language is a critique of existing reality and established human orders. Third, the redescription that expresses religious hope is according to unexpected and unformulable possibilities, because any complete account of the human condition includes experiences, such as death, which baffle talk and block action. On the grounds of the mystery it meets in its vertical dimension, religious language in its horizontal dimension appeals to the unexpected gift and the unformulable future.

Religious language, therefore, provides a kind of relational model, from which those who know the notation may read a redescription of human experience and worldly reality according to possibilities grounded in the transcendent.

Its functioning implies truth claims, but the making of truth claims does not allow us to interpret religious language as a factual description of existing reality when taken as including supernatural entities. It has sometimes been interpreted that way, and for that reason religious myth became a prison from which men and women had to be liberated. But even though myth is concerned with the integration of human experience in contrast to parable, which functions to shatter our expectations and underline the limitations of every order we devise (Crossan, 1975), myth itself is still properly understood dynamically as referring to the future and its possibilities rather than to the present and its structure.

The merely factual, even when understood supernaturally, is the destruction of every genuine religious meaning. Openness to the transcendent becomes on the level of human experience openness to the future and to its unformulable possibilities.

The merely factual is also the destruction of any genuine politics. When the utopian element is banished, when in public life there is a fear of the imagination and a refusal to consider truly new possibilities because of their incalculability, then politicians become just front-men for experts and social technology replaces politics as the ordering element in society. *De factis non disputatur*, ran the Scholastic adage. That is why politics is not about facts but about possibilities.

7

Pluralism, privacy and the interior self

'Do not you believe that there is in man a "deep" so profound as to be hidden even to him in whom it is?' The words are St Augustine's in his *Expositions on the Book of Psalms* (1848, II: 194). The self for Augustine was, as Thomas Prufer puts it, a 'transphenomenal abyss' (1963: 6). We enter the depths of that interior self helped by the light of God. 'Being admonished by all this to return to myself', Augustine writes in the *Confessions*, 'I entered into my own depths with You as guide; and I was able to do it because You were my helper. I entered, and with the eye of my soul, such as it was, I saw Your unchangeable Light shining over that same eye of my soul, over my mind' (1943: 137). For Augustine, to quote Thomas Prufer again, 'The self is constituted in listening and speaking to God; it is no longer primarily constituted as a being in the world' (1963: 6). In Augustine we have the exemplary instance at the beginning of Western culture of the Christian experience of the interior self as standing alone in the presence of God. The individual has his or her self-identity in a relationship with God in interiority. In other words, the person is constituted as an interior or transphenomenal individual self by being present to God in inward solitude.

I myself have written in my book *Body As Spirit* about the problem created by the non-worldliness of that conception of the self. The Christian acknowledgement of the individual was a valuable contribution to the emergence of human freedom, and that individuality was achieved by the interiority of an inward relationship with God. But the interior self of Christian tradition not merely transcends the world, but is also alienated from it, and the cleavage between the interior self and the phenomenal world has been harmful. It led eventually to the modern isolated ego, with its loneliness and prome-thean individualism. In *Body As Spirit* I was chiefly concerned with the refusal of bodiliness. Here I should like more directly to consider the relation of the individual, interior self to society. To do so, I will take up again Habermas's theory of religion, because in it he relates the history of religion to the question of social identity.

Habermas distinguishes four stages of social evolution in regard to ego and group identity (Habermas and Heinrich, 1974: 25–84; Habermas 1974b: 91–103).

The first stage was that of archaic societies. Their structure was determined by kinship ties. These provided the basis for the elaboration of mythical world-views. Analogies were made among all natural and cultural phenomena and expressed in mythical images by using kinship relationships as an interpretative schema. The myth thus produced an il-lusion of order by assigning a meaningful place to every per-ceptible element. Almost every contingency was interpreted away in that fashion. Archaic society was very insecure because of the under-development of its productive forces and the lack of control over the environment. The insecurity was dissolved by the myth. Since in the world of myth all entities are analogues, men do not essentially differ from the things of nature, nor does the tribe stand out from its individual mem-bers or from nature. At this stage, therefore, problems of iden-tity do not arise.

Problems come at the second stage, the world of the poly-theistic religions of the early civilizations. These civilizations have a centralized political organization, either kingdom or city-state, which requires legitimation. Hence the polity has to be taken up into the religious narratives and made firm through ritual. At this stage, nature begins to be desacralized, and the political institutions receive a degree of autonomy in relation to the cosmic order. The effect is to open up an area of the unaccountable, where contingencies can no longer be interpreted away as with the myth of the previous stage, but where the individual has to act to bring the situation under control. It is at this stage that the gods assume human form and are conceived as actively and sometimes arbitrarily inter-vening in human affairs. The individual faced with unaccountable contingencies established patterns of interaction with the gods by devising new forms of religious action, such as prayer, sacrifice and worship. What we therefore observe at this stage is the emergence of the individual in self-identity from the universal complex of other entities and, at the same time, the distinction of the particular concrete community from the universality of the cosmic order. Nevertheless, religious adherence is still identified with membership of a particular political community. For that reason, the particular community can become distinct from the universality of the cosmic order on the one hand and from singular individuals on the other, without that destroying the unity of the world centred in it and the social identity thus created. So, an equilibrium was achieved, a unity in difference, relating individuality, particularity and universality. There was a limitation, however. The absolute right of the individual had not yet been established.

With the universal religions, from which Habermas takes Christianity as the exemplar, we reach the third stage. 'The one, the other-worldly, all-knowing and wholly just and gracious God of Christendom', writes Habermas, 'leads to the forming of an ego-identity severed from all concrete roles and norms. This "I" can know itself as a completely individuated being' (1974b: 93). The individual standing before God becomes free and of infinite worth. Furthermore, because the commands of God are universal, the bearer of religion is no longer the particular political group, but the community of believers, to which all men potentially belong. Here, then, we have the emergence of the singular individual, considered of infinite worth, in a potentially universal community. However, the political systems of the time of the universal religions, which is the stage of the high civilizations, were class societies with extreme inequalities of power and wealth. For that reason they were in great need of powerful legitimation, but the universalism of the monotheistic religions militated against their giving such legitimation. 'At this stage', says Habermas, 'the religious meaning systems and the political imperatives of self-maintenance become structurally incompatible' (*ibid.*). Ideology entered in to ease this conflict. Its function was to cover over the dissimilarity between the collective identity as tied to the particular State and the individual ego-identity formed by the universal religious community.

That problem of identity is inherent in all the high civilizations, but it remained latent until modern times because of various mechanisms that mediated between the political order and religious universalism. Habermas mentions three such mediating mechanisms. First, the persistence of earlier identity formations, derived from myth and magic. Second, the distinction made between the members of the community of believers and those still to be converted. This distinction was used to justify the treatment of political enemies as though they were outside the boundary of the universal religious community. Third – and this was the chief factor – the dualism set up between divine transcendence, represented by the Church, and the secular world, represented by the State.

In the modern era, which constitutes the fourth stage of social evolution, the mediating mechanisms have lost their efficacy. To take each of the three in turn. Protestantism eliminated many of the pre-Christian elements that had been incorporated into the Catholic order. The sifting out of anachronistic, pagan elements increased the pressure towards strongly universalistic imperatives and the individualized ego-structures corresponding to them. Again, with the break-up of the one Catholic Church into a multitude of confessions and denominations, membership of the community of believers ceased to be an exclusive and rigidly institutional attribute. The principle of toleration and the voluntary nature of religious association became generally acknowledged. Finally, Habermas takes note of the fact that recent theology has moved to overcome the traditional dualism between the Church and the world by giving a this-worldly interpretation of salvation.

On that last point, Habermas, in commenting upon what he calls 'the repoliticization of the biblical inheritance observable in contemporary theological discussion', argues that the idea of a personal God cannot be salvaged in the process, although he admits that the new interpretation does not mean 'atheism in the sense of a liquidation without trace of the idea of God'. What, then, does he think it means? He writes:

The idea of God is transformed [*aufgehoben*] into the concept of a *Logos* that determines the community of believers and the real life-context of a self-emancipating society. 'God' becomes the name for a communicative structure that forces men, on pain of a loss of their humanity, to go beyond their accidental, empirical nature to encounter one another *indirectly*, that is, across an objective something that they themselves are not (1976a: 121 – Habermas's italics).

The theologians in question might respond: Has Habermas probed the implications of that communicative structure deeply enough?

To understand Habermas's account of the history of religion, one must recall his thesis that the cultural life of societies is not a random process, but follows a rationally reconstructible pattern of development. His argument for this is an interlocking series of considerations. To speak in general terms, social systems are engaged in a double process of exchange. There is, first, the appropriation of outer nature, namely the non-human environment, through production and, second, the appropriation of inner nature, which means human material, through socialization. The adaptation of inner nature to society in socialization is what is meant by cultural life. The adaptation or socialization is brought about through the medium of normative structures, in which human needs are interpreted and various actions allowed or made obligatory. Because normative structures are thus the means of socialization, the social integration of inner nature marches in step with normative claims that call for justification. But the discursive redemption of normative claims follows a rational sequence.

Since socialization is dependent upon normative claims and their justification, it itself follows a rational pattern. In other words, the cultural life of society is directional and embodies an irreversible sequence. The development of science and technology manifests, according to Habermas, an inner logic with rational sequences fixed from the outset, so that, as long as the continuity of tradition is not broken, cognitive advances cannot be forgotten and every deviation from the irreversible line of advance is experienced as a regression. Likewise, for him normative claims and their justification follow an inner logic, which creates an irreversible line of development, so that, as long as the continuity of tradition is unbroken, socially attained stages of moral consciousness cannot be forgotten and any deviation is experienced as a regression.

What, then, is the rationally reconstructible pattern of development in the cultural life of social systems? The question can be put in another way: What is the inner logic of the development of world-views? There is an increasing demand for the discursive redemption of normative claims, which leads from myth through religion to philosophy and ideology and thence to critique. In the directional process the following irreversible trends are discernible: the expansion of the secular in relation to the sacred; the movement from heteronomy to autonomy; the evacuation of cognitive contents from world-views, so that cosmology is replaced by a pure system of morality; the shift from tribal particularism to universalistic and individualized orientation; increasing reflexivity of the mode of belief (1976a: 11–12).

The last trend is the determining one. Döbert, a younger collaborator of Habermas, to whose work Habermas refers, interprets the history of religious consciousness as the development of a process of reflection through which human beings gain clarity in regard to themselves and free themselves from the domination of normative systems that impose themselves with a nature-like compulsion (1973: 140). Since the opposite of a nature-like compulsion of norms is a mutual agreement on norms, reached in a free reciprocal process of communication, Döbert suggests that the development of religion may be viewed as the evolution of communicative competence. The end-point of this development of religion as communicative competence is described by Peukert in summing up both Habermas and Döbert (1976: 228). Persons as subjects will have become competent to test and render perspicuous for one another assertions and behavioural expectations through a linguistically mediated process of reciprocal reflexivity. Thus, the final stage or ideal is the reciprocal transparency of persons in a process of communication.

To return now to the modern era as the fourth stage in Habermas's account of the evolution of social identity. The considerations I have been outlining should make understandable why Habermas contends that at this stage all that is left of the universal religions is the core of a universalistic morality. (The mystical components, grounded in a contemplative experience that is characterized by a withdrawal from action, cannot be taken up (*aufgehoben*) into ethics and have split off into a sphere of their own (1976b: 101).) The consequence of this clarification and purification of the universalistic structures originally introduced by the world religions is a cleavage between the ego-identity derived from universalistic structures and collective identity as bound up with a particular community. Habermas writes:

on the basis of universalistic norms no particular entity possessing an identity-forming power (such as the family, the tribe, the city, state or nation) can set up bounds to demarcate itself from alien groups. Rather, the 'own' group is here replaced by the category of 'the other' who is no longer conceived as an outsider because of his non-membership (1974b: 94).

Somehow particular citizenship or national identity has to be enlarged into a cosmopolitan or universal identity. But how? The whole of mankind is an abstraction. Unless there can be found an all-embracing collective identity on the basis of which individualized ego-identities can be formed, then universalistic morality and the ego-structures that go with it will remain a mere postulate, actualized only occasionally and then within the private sphere, without in a substantial fashion grounding social life.

Needless to say, Habermas does not see any solution in a return to religion. For him Christianity, though the most rational of the religions, is no longer viable after its confrontation with science and secular morality. But further, during the Christian era the opposition between the universalistic ego-structures and the particularism of the State was covered over, not resolved. He examines the solution offered by Hegel, who remains for Habermas a contemporary thinker precisely because he gave the impulse to reflection upon the problem of identity.

An adequate presentation of Hegel's solution would require an account of his general philosophy, because he viewed the problem of identity, namely the cleavage between the singular 'I' and the particular society, in the context of the self-unfolding of absolute Spirit in nature and history.

But it must be enough here to say that Hegel defended the thesis that modern society finds its rational identity in the sovereign constitutional State, which, though particular, was for him the embodiment of universal morality. Few would disagree with Habermas when he argues against Hegel that the modern State cannot provide a rational identity, uniting the singular, the particular and the universal. Two of the reasons he gives may be mentioned. First, the modern State remains a class-structure; it does not embody the universalizable interests of the whole people, but organizes the domination of group interests over the whole. Second, recent developments, such as nuclear weapons, multi-national corporations, world-wide communication, have rendered the sovereign territorial State anachronistic.

The failure of Hegel indicates for Habermas that the old social identity, centred in the State and both articulated and fixed in particular traditions and world-images, is now finally outdated and irrelevant. He goes on to outline a new identity, which he contends is possible in the complex societies of today and at the same time compatible with a universalistic ego-structure.

This new identity is not tied to State boundaries; it is not related to a particular territory or organization. It does not come from membership in some permanent collective body. It is grounded, Habermas says,

in the consciousness of universal and equal chances to participate in the kind of communication processes by which identity formation becomes a continuous learning process. Here the individual is no longer confronted by collective identity as a traditional authority, as a fixed objectivity on the basis of which self-identity can be built. Rather, individuals are the participants in the shaping of the collective will underlying the design of a common identity (1974b: 99).

He discerns in present societies processes of communication concerning norms and values. These processes are often not institutionalized politically, and are therefore in that sense sub-political. But in fact they penetrate and affect the political system and political decisions. The consciousness of a universal and equal opportunity to participate in the social formation of norms and values is the basis for a new collective identity, uniting the singular, the particular and the universal. This new identity of a still-emerging global society cannot be articulated in world-images. It presupposes the validity of universalistic moral systems, but these can be grounded simply upon the norms inherent in rational discourse. Habermas is here referring to his own analysis of the normative basis of communicative action. This leads him to say of the new identity:

Such an identity no longer requires fixed contents. Those interpretations which make man's situation in today's world comprehensible are distinguished from the traditional world images not so much in that they are more limited in scope, but in that their status is open to counter-arguments and revisions at any time (*ibid.*, 100).

I have already said enough about Habermas's dismissal of religion to make it unnecessary here to discuss his theory of identity from that standpoint. Instead, I want to take up what I consider his valuable insights on social identity into a theological context. I think they can help us reflect upon Christian identity today and the problems related to that.

Does not what Habermas says about identity correspond to an experience undergone by an increasing number of Christians today? I mean the breakdown of the old Christian identity and the emergence of a new identity. Many, I think, no longer find their social identity as Christians in membership of a particular Christian Church standing over against them as a collective body with a traditional authority. They still regard themselves as Christians, but their identity as Christians comes to them as participants with others in a continuous collective process of learning to be Christians. They are not Christians because they have joined themselves to a fixed, already existent Christian collectivity, with requirements for membership clearly defined so as to provide an objective basis for the Christian self-identity of individuals. They remain Christians, despite perhaps the irregularity, tenuousness or even non-existence of their connection with a particular Church, because they continue to participate in the social process of shaping what it means to be a Christian at the present time. They are engaged with others in forming Christian norms and values in the context of the situation today.

Admittedly, most Christians still find themselves within one or other of the different Christian Churches, just as everyone is still a citizen of a particular State. But the meaning of Church membership as that of citizenship has changed. Citizenship in a particular State is no longer the basis for self-identity in contemporary society. We are participants in a world-wide process in which, with others from various countries as equal participants, we are striving for a new collective identity. Our fundamental social identity comes from our conscious share in shaping the new, emergent collective will. Our present citizenship is a point of entry into the wider process, a place from which we may act, and it may indeed recede right into the background if we are working with citizens from many countries in some international body or movement. It is likewise with Church membership. It is no longer fundamental as a fixed, objective basis on which we define our self-identity as Christians. That is now given through participation in ongoing Christian history. At most Church membership serves as a point of entry into the Christian process, a place from which we may act, and it recedes more and more into the background as we develop a network of relationships with others that ignore the boundaries of particular Churches. People sometimes hardly know how to answer when they are asked whether they are members of a particular Church. The reason is simply that membership is no longer a useful or relevant concept in defining social identity.

As soon as social identity is seen as given by active and conscious participation in a history and not by membership of a fixed, objective, authoritative collectivity, the question of pluralism and religious diversity is thrown into a new light. I will begin with a consideration of pluralism as a political factor (see Davis, 1974).

John Courtney Murray defined pluralism as: 'the coexistence within the political community of groups who hold divergent views with regard to ultimate questions concerning the nature and destiny of man' (1954: 165). Pluralism in that sense may be called valuational pluralism, because divergent views concerning the nature and destiny of man both arise from and lead to differing and incompatible value judgements. The problem of pluralism for the political community and its common action lies in the divergent value judgements governing decisions.

Pluralism implies disagreement and dissension within the political community. But one cannot speak of pluralism unless there is one community. Pluralism, then, also implies unity, some consensus or agreement. The divergent groups form one community; they agree to live together and co-operate in action for common goals. Pluralism is not brute plurality. It means harmony amid discord, unity of social life and political action amid religious and valuational conflict.

Pluralism is of the very essence of politics. Herbert Richardson, as I have already mentioned, distinguishes between non-political and political societies on the basis of the refusal or admission of pluralism. Political societies are structurally pluralist, in as much as they aim at a co-willing that unifies divergent willings, while keeping their divergent plurality (*Religion and Political Society*, 1974: 103). The exclusion of pluralism is thus the suppression of the properly political dimension of society.

But how can a society deal in a rational manner with divergent value judgements? Without a disastrous dehumanization, it cannot evade the issue by ignoring values, though that is the direction taken by contemporary technocratic society. Again, if those in power simply assert their own values and impose them in practice, there is a destruction of human freedom and a virtual elimination of politics. If neither evasion nor absolutism, what then? Herbert Richardson makes what I consider a too-facile distinction between procedural and teleological values, but his account does point in the right direction. There can be pluralism only when people agree to engage in open and continuing discussion. 'Civilization', wrote Thomas Gilby as quoted by John Courtney Murray, 'is formed by men locked together in argument. From this dialogue the community becomes a political community' (Murray, 1960: 6). As I myself wrote in an essay on pluralism:

There should be a public deliberation about values, through which the implications and consequences of divergent value judgements are comprehensively displayed. The supposition is that open and adequate deliberation will favour the occurrence of correct value judgements on the part of men of good will and thus create a sound public consensus. A pluralist society allows dissent. It does not, however, exclude, but rather as a human society or community of meaning presupposes a consensus, created and maintained freely in open discussion. A public consensus will not eliminate dissent; indeed, as a freely created agreement, it presupposes and implies dissent. But dissent is identified as dissent with reference to the consensus, and a minimum of consensus is a condition for political argument. Political argument is not just the attempted provoking of assent to intellectually cogent reasoning, but a common process of deliberation, evaluation and decision (Davis, 1974: 247).

What Habermas, it seems to me, has added to considerations such as those is the insight that the particular political communities or States do not provide an appropriate embodiment of the common process of reaching agreement about norms and values. First, the existing States are all structures of domination, objectified disvalues, so that the pursuit of genuine values will be a rejection of the present political order. Membership of a State is, therefore, part of the contingent facticity of one's existence, not a definition of one's normative being as a moral and social agent. Second, all the determining social and political issues of today transcend the boundaries of particular States. Human history has become one in a conscious and active way, so that a social identity that is not anachronistic has to be grounded upon a collective reality wider than that of the particular State. There is, indeed, not yet a universal, global order, but there is the opportunity of participating in its emergence by evoking the inherently universal structure of communication to shape a new collective will, leading to an order beyond the present divisions. However much we may positively value a particular national heritage, possessing it as a fixed and finished whole cannot ground a rational social identity today. Instead, that heritage must serve as a source of a distinctive contribution to the common enterprise of forming a new, complex and universal identity for people of all nations.

I am reminded here of Lonergan's concept of cosmopolis. In dealing with the problem of cultural decline, he argues:

What is necessary is a cosmopolis that is neither class nor state, that stands above all their claims, that cuts them down to size, that is founded on the native detachment and disinterestedness of every intelligence, that commands man's first allegiance, that implements itself primarily through that allegiance, that is too universal to be bribed, too impalpable to be forced, too effective to be ignored (1958: 238).

'Cosmopolis', he adds, 'is above all politics. So far from being rendered superfluous by a successful World Government, it would be all the more obviously needed to offset the tendencies of that and any other government to be shortsightedly practical' (*ibid.*, 239).

I do not share Lonergan's confidence in detached intelligence as the cure for human ills. He sees cosmopolis as counteracting the tendency to identify the rational with the immediately practical or expedient. But even that tendency is met better by the active universalism of an interest in human liberation than by detached reflection. The worst expedients of the modern technocrats are cloaked by a claim to the detached objectivity of science. Intelligence is as biased or as universalistic as one's practical life; it is neither unfallen nor separately redeemed. Further, Lonergan has a low view of politics as merely concerned with the exercise of power and the sustaining of law and order. But a political community in the full sense comes into existence when men engage in civilized debate concerning the ends of life and of society.

To put my point briefly: social change is not brought about by a change of consciousness alone, but by a concurrence of a change of consciousness and a change of structures. Cosmopolis registers the change of consciousness when it places our first allegiance beyond class or State. What needs to be added is active participation in the formation of new, universal structures. It is that active participation that grounds a new social identity.

In their writings, both Lonergan and Habermas, in my opinion, exaggerate the function of detached, discursive rationality as exemplified by science, at the expense of other forms of rationality. But the problem of pluralism cannot be met by communication solely at the theoretical level. That becomes abundantly clear when we turn to the question of religious diversity.

I have said that a basic Christian identity today is not

grounded upon membership in a particular Church, but upon participation in an ongoing, and therefore future-oriented, Christian history. I now want to argue that that account itself is a limited view. Christian identity is but one mode or manifestation of a more fundamental religious identity, which we share with people from other religious traditions, as all being participants in a single total history. That history is now entering a new phase, in which this fundamental religious identity, previously implicit and indeed blocked and denied, is now emerging.

That conviction is based on several different but convergent considerations (Smith, 1976: *passim*).

First, past religious history is not fully intelligible unless it is understood as a single history of human religiousness. Not merely are many developments similar across the different traditions, but also the actual histories of the different religious communities are much more intertwined than previous accounts, written from the viewpoint of a single tradition, have allowed. The point has readily been admitted in regard to the East and the overlapping of Confucianism, Taoism and Buddhism in China, but Wilfred Cantwell Smith has shown how Christians and Muslims have to a large extent shared the same history. In a recent article he states:

my thesis is that both Christian history and Islamic history are to be understood in significant part as each a sub-sector of a history of human religiousness that is in principle, of course, world-wide and history-long, but for our present purposes must be seen as at least a context of development that we may call Islamo-Christian history (1977: 519).

To apply that thesis to two particular phenomena: Scholasticism and what we may call Scripturalism. A true historical apprehension would see 'Islamic thought and Jewish and Christian, more or less in that order so far as beginnings go, participating historically in a Mediterranean movement of thought called scholasticism' (*ibid.*, 520). Again:

when seen on a world scale, Jews, Christians, and Muslims may all be understood, and understood more tellingly, as participating historically in the religious phenomenon of Scripturalism – initiating their participation in the Scripture movement at somewhat different stages in its dynamic development, with interesting and important differential results; but the phenomenon of Scripture in no one of the cases can be so fully and accurately understood as when apprehended in all (*ibid.*).

Second, religious exclusiveness is itself a particular development that arose at a particular time and place and would now seem to have come to the end of its historical usefulness. Smith writes:

It has certainly been true for some time now and for considerable parts of the world that men have their life religiously in independent, even isolationist, communities, separated from each other not absolutely, of course, but in principle, and even considerably so in practice. Our new study of mankind's religiousness, however, is investigating the fact that this situation arose in human development. In *The Meaning and End of Religion* I have suggested that it arose at a given time and place – in Western Asia, in that fascinatingly creative period between Alexander and Muhammad – and has since established itself, and has spread, though not to all the world: to India quite late, and to China virtually never. We in the West have come to take it so utterly for granted that religious life should be lived out in separated and boundaried communities, that we have given less attention than it deserves to the great question of how this came to be and what it implies. Yet one is beginning to discern perhaps a total history of man's religiousness, constituting a pattern in which the rise of the separated religious communities constitutes a meaningful episode (1976: 109).

Third, there is discernible today a convergence of religious traditions, which is in a fair way to transform all of them. That does not mean that all religious traditions are saying the same thing or that there is no religious truth or that anything goes in matters of religion. The history of religion is not just a history of authentic religious experience and achievement, but of religious aberration. A work of discernment and purification is needed, and this will include judgements of truth or falsity, though it must be remembered that such judgements have to take account of the figurative nature of religious expression.

What, however, is implied by this development is – to return by another route to the point of my first chapter – the end of orthodoxy, in the sense of a religious identity mediated through the fixed, objectified contents of a particular religious tradition. There may indeed be invariant elements, but it is not possible to forestall future history and draw a clear line between the invariant and the variable elements. Thus, as I wrote elsewhere:

It is possible that the Christian tradition has a central, decisive contribution to make in world history. However, to put forward a *prior* claim of that kind savours of ethnocentricity and cultural imperialism. It also runs up against serious difficulties of hermeneutic or epistemological principle, because in effect it attempts to bypass the mediation of history and *praxis* in our coming to the truth. Only in the actual process of the emergence of world order shall we be able to discern the precise role of existing elements (1976: 103).

I conclude, then, that basic religious identity – at least for some of us – is not given by belonging to a particular religious tradition, but by active participation in the present shaping of a universality to be realized in the future. Present working for a yet-to-be-realized universality can already unite people of different positions (Habermas, 1974b: 103).

The structure of communication now growing among the religious communities with their traditions is not just a matter of theoretical or doctrinal discussion. It is a sharing of life. People are learning to live together, to listen to one another's stories, to interpret and become familiar with alien symbols, to respect different customs and join in the rites of others. There are different degrees of sharing. Sometimes, as often in the past, an element from one tradition is assimilated into other traditions so fully that its origin is forgotten, though it may well be substantially modified in the process. At other times, the sharing takes place in a manner that does not destroy, but perhaps heightens the sense of difference. There is developing religiously what Herbert Richardson, with reference to politics, calls a 'polyconsciousness', namely, a more highly differentiated consciousness with a greater capacity of bearing plurality within itself. 'A person', he writes, 'living in a political society must possess more power of empathy; he must be an Empathetic Man. Such empathetic persons are able to identify imaginatively with those who are different from themselves and, in this way, to bear a higher degree of inward contrariety' (*Religion and Political Society*, 1974: 113).

It must be added that religious pluralism, when placed in the context of universal communication, is not an evil to be eliminated, but the appropriate expression of the transcendence of the religious object, of human freedom and of the historical mediation of human truth and value. The universalistic structure of religious identity as I have outlined it does not anticipate the removal of plurality, but articulates a unity of communication in the lasting differences of historical experience and remembrance and consequently of traditions, though these remain under a constant process of development and revision. Traditions with their diversity will never be replaced by the abstract universality of formal rational discourse.

Though Habermas would no doubt disagree, I see the basic religious identity I have described as coinciding with the new social identity he has analysed, though articulating it at a deeper level. Previously, in agreement with Peukert, I argued that communicative action had implications demanding religious expression. In a similar way, I contend here that the new universal identity now emerging is a new articulation, beyond particularism and orthodoxy, of the religious identity of the past, not its abolition without remainder.

According to both Hegel and Habermas, it was monotheism, particularly in its Christian form, which led to the emergence of the singular individual. Standing before God, the 'I' became a completely individuated being, possessing an unconditional or infinite worth apart from any particular concrete role. The singular individual, therefore, had his or her social identity in a potentially universal community of believers rather than from the State. When Habermas, however, turns to the problem of identity in modern society, he does not take up Hegel's concern for the estrangement of modern man from the Absolute. I also find nothing in Habermas's account of the new social identity to replace the function of monotheism in grounding a singular ego-structure. Participation in communication processes for the formation of norms and values is a basis for a universalistic ego-structure, transcending the particularism of enclosed groups. But such a universalistic ego-structure does not of itself imply the unconditional worth of the individual. Are we then simply to relinquish the Christian stress upon the individual self? After all, the doctrine of an individual self, distinct from God but constituted in relationship with him, is not shared by the non-theistic religious traditions.

Political theology is in part a protest against the virtual confinement of religion since the Enlightenment to the private sphere of the individual and the family. Metz, for example, proclaimed a programme of deprivatization (*Entprivatisierung*). He presented political theology in contrast to existentialist, personalist and transcendental theologies, which for him have compounded the tendency to privatization. As a theologian Metz began his career as a disciple of Rahner and an interpreter of his transcendental theology. Rahner's theological anthropology takes the transcendental experience of the subject as its starting-point and context of meaning. Metz turned away from this towards a theological eschatology, for which the political subject was the starting-point and context of meaning (Mann, 1969–70).

There are, I think, several distinct issues entangled here. I should like to try to unravel them.

Religion as a private affair or privatized religion may be taken to mean a religious outlook and practice solely concerned with the personal values of private life. The social and political factors of life in the world are left unexamined. These are considered as outside one's personal life, even though they constitute the world in which one has to earn one's living. Religion, however, is a personal matter. Its concern is with my attitudes and my behaviour as immediately bearing upon my personal relationships with the other members of my family and with people I personally meet. The function of religion is to encourage values and behaviour that promote harmony in interpersonal relationships and to foster generosity and helpfulness. As for the misfortunes of life, these are to be met with patient endurance, supported by the thought of the transitoriness of this life and the rewards of the next. At the same time, a genuine sense of the transcendent may frequently prevent this kind of religion from becoming entirely self-enclosed, and a thrust towards the transcendent remains there as a potentially disturbing element. Within the context of privatized religion, however, the sense of the transcendent is chiefly nurtured through individual prayer. The devout strive to develop an interior or spiritual life by setting aside time for mental prayer and practising other spiritual techniques.

Clearly such a religion is too limited in range to counteract the injustices of existing society or to create a free society. For that reason the whole concept of an interior or spiritual life has fallen into disrepute among some. But what has happened here both in privatized religion and in the reaction against it is a confusion between the interior self and the private self.

The interior self emerges as a result of a differentiation of consciousness, which was first achieved religiously when the individual self was constituted in relation to God. The subject or self with God was differentiated as an interior world over against the external world. Later the relation with God was dropped or ignored, and Christian interiority became modern subjectivity. In either case, the interior self is the subject as distinctly aware of his or her individual being and activity as a conscious subject.

The private self, in contrast, is the self as acting within the private sphere, even when not particularly self-aware. The private sphere consists in those relatively unorganized segments of life, notably the family, still existing in the interstices of bureaucratically administered society. In the trend towards the totally administered society, the family and the related areas of individually chosen personal activities fall more and more under the indirect or hidden control of bureaucratic bodies, such as those that constitute the entertainment industry. Further, because of the dependence of the private sphere upon the public, the sense of freedom in one's private life is to a large extent illusory. Nevertheless, the private sphere does remain a place where people feel a release from the relentless rational routines and compulsions of their working lives.

To confine religion to the private sphere, so that it serves as a therapeutic counterbalance on Sunday to the grinding rationality of the rest of the week, with the Church as the rallying point for the suburban escape of family life from factory and city, is blatantly to distort it. But the effect upon religion is derivative. It is chiefly human beings who are crippled when offered personal fulfilment only in the private sphere, so that their freedom is effectively curtailed to a consumer and recreational freedom. Human persons are in that way being refused the full realization of their subjectivity, which comes

only in building a truly human society in a free and equal communication with other human persons. Thus, the call for the
deprivatization of religion and theology would be more adequately expressed as an element in a demand for the deprivatization of the personal life of human subjects.

The underlying problem here is positivism and the Romantic compromise with positivism. What is at work in the present
polarity between public and private spheres is a positivistic
identification of rationality with the supposedly value-free,
formal rationality of the empirical–analytic sciences. That
identification excludes any rational grounding of norms and
values, so that the ethical and the religious are put outside the
realm of the rational and assigned to pre-rational conventions
or irrational free decisions. Romantic and, at a later date,
existentialist theologies and philosophies have compromised
with positivism, in so far as they too have placed faith and
moral decision beyond reason and rational assessment. The
polarization between the scientifically (or, more accurately,
scientistically) rational and the existential as irrational is reflected in the present configuration of public and private. What is
admissible in the public sphere must be justifiable through the
value-free procedures of science and technology, which
means that public affairs are, or at least should be, in the hands
of experts. Values are relegated to the private sphere, because
they are not subject to rational grounding or control. I myself
once heard a sociologist argue that the discussion of values
had no place in a university, because no hard knowledge on
them was available; they should be discussed over beer on a
Friday night at the faculty club. There are some who see the
pocket of irrationality, represented by the private sphere, as
eventually overcome when improved techniques enable the irrational to be fully controlled rationally.

The deprivatization advocated by political theology, if not
illusory, must be the overcoming of the polarity between the
rational and the existential, between public knowledge and
strategic action on the one hand and private faith and voluntary involvement on the other. Political theology cannot be
simply the inclusion of a concern with social and political
issues into a structure of theological thought that remains pri-
vatistic. It must articulate and defend a wider concept of

rationality than that of the positivists, so that norms and values, moral and religious, can be recognized as subject to the procedures and criteria of an intersubjective communication and a prudential or practical rationality. Political theology must become critical theology, in order to be a public theology, operative within the public sphere. That indeed implies that moral and religious assertions are always open to counter-arguments and revisions. Theology, however, does not become political by using social and political issues as material with which to exercise and articulate an utterly private, incommunicable and therefore socially impotent, existential conviction. It does so by entering and submitting itself to public discussion.

The overcoming of the polarity between the public and private spheres does not however mean the suppression or desuetude of interiority. On the contrary, it will be the liberation of the interior self. The interior self is the self-conscious subject in possession of his or her individuated being and activities and thus through self-possession is free. Such a self is the political subject *par excellence*, capable of entering into the communication process among free participants which constitutes the political life of society as distinct from its mere administration. There is no politics without individuated persons or interior selves and, on the other hand, the self remains undeveloped unless it enters into political relationship with others. By politics I mean the collective shaping of norms and values in free communication, not the struggle for and distribution of power in society.

It is a mistake to confuse the acknowledgement of the unconditional worth of the individual with the individualism of bourgeois society. Bourgeois individualism reduces human beings to their economic relationships and, in doing so, puts them in competition with one another. This ignores all differences among men and women except one, and that one is basically a merely quantitative variation in the amount of property. Society is organized on the principle that human beings are replaceable units, shaped to fit into a limited number of functional slots. There is no place for the immense variety of individual qualities and personal creativity, for that would disturb the system. Individualism is thus not respect for the individuated being of the free person, but simply the human unrelatedness of men and women when organized solely in terms of economic competition. Paradoxically, therefore, individualism means conformity not individuality.

For that reason, a recent writer, Ronald Massanari, has suggested that the theologies of play or imagination – he has in mind the writings of Harvey Cox, Sam Keen, David L. Miller and others – should be counted among the theologies of liberation. These 'playful theologies' are concerned with the liberation of the white American middle-class male from the dominant myth of his oppressive society. He writes:

In the dominant 'myth' great emphasis is placed on individualism as part of its ideal. But a closer look shows that individualism is really a closed conformity to the ideal of the 'myth'. In actual fact the individualism of the 'myth' is the death of the individual. Its affect [*sic*] is militant conformity. When playful theology refers to the individual it is not bound to the conformities of the 'myth'. It undercuts the very form of individualism found in this monovision of the dominant class, thus potentially liberating the individual to be a creative, self-inventing person (1977: 202).

The theologies of play as liberation theologies thus urge us to see play as well as work, celebration as well as routine, imagination as well as reason as part of politics when understood in a fully human way. The joyful festivities promoted by religion and the imaginative richness of its symbolic ritual and art are wrongly dismissed as anodynes; they are rather signs of a full humanity. The sombre and humourless seriousness of much Marxism is one of the clearest signs that some important element has been missed.

Is not that element perhaps the element of transcendence? Can the interior self in the sense of the individuated and self-possessed human subject be constituted and sustained otherwise than in a relationship to the transcendent?

Herbert Richardson maintains, as I have previously mentioned, that political society in the sense of a structurally pluralist society rests upon faith in the transcendent, a faith which prevents the establishment of any official religion and excludes the absolutizing of any single set of temporal goals. Further, he sees the uniqueness of every person as one of the ways in which transcendence has been given expression in the

Judaeo-Christian tradition. 'To affirm the uniqueness of persons means not simply that God transcends and is uniquely different from every other person, but that all created persons transcend and are uniquely different from one another' (*Religion and Political Society*, 1974: 117). He adds: 'This means that there must exist a realm of personal relation and human privacy that stands quite free from scientific – or even social – manipulation' (*ibid.*).

This suggests another and deeper concept of privacy than the one previously examined. For me – I am not attributing this thesis to Richardson – personal privacy at its most intimate coincides with the mystical element in religion. By the mystical element I mean the experience and subsequent conviction that at its deepest core the reality of my individual self becomes one with Ultimate Reality. I have chosen a general formulation. I have made it clear elsewhere (Davis, 1976: 59–86) that I do not consider negligible the difference between a mystical oneness that preserves the distinction of a personal God and the individual human being and a mystical oneness that identifies the self and Ultimate Reality without distinction. I also think that theism has made possible the emergence of the individual self in a way that other forms of religion have not. Nevertheless, the mystical element as found in all the major religions establishes for each person a private space where his intimate being opens out on to a reality that transcends history, the temporal order and society; where, therefore, time is intersected by eternity. In doing so, it liberates the human person into a subjective freedom beyond the conventions of any particular social order.

Clearly, in one sense, that mystical element is apolitical. As transcendent, it is not enclosed within the political order. But I suggest that it is eminently political in as much as it is the deepest source and ground of politics. In releasing human persons into individual freedom as subjects, it makes possible the process of communication among free and equal participants, which is the essence of emancipated politics. The preservation of genuine politics against the encroachment of administration by experts depends upon the continued survival of the individual in our society. But if the human subject has no transcendent and indefeasibly private core, it is hard to see why the individual as a social factor should not be abolished as an obsolete historical form as the scientific control of social systems becomes comprehensive and more efficient.

To adapt, then, a remark of Horkheimer, without the mystical element politics is mere business. If it ignores that mystical element or fails to integrate it with the rational, political theology will be insufficiently critical in its assessment of the present situation and will end by being just one more coat of varnish over post-Enlightenment theology, instead of its replacement.

Notes

1 The change from a classicist notion of culture to an empirical notion of culture and the effect of this change upon belief and theology are a recurrent theme in Bernard Lonergan's writings. See, for example, two essays in *A Second Collection* (1974): 'Belief: today's issue' (87–99) and 'Revolution in Catholic theology' (231–8).

2 See the book of Maritain entitled *Humanisme intégral*, published in 1936. University of Notre Dame Press has issued a reprint (1973) of the English translation. In the Preface (vii) to that reprint reference is made to Pope Paul VI's citation of Maritain.

3 In talking of 'mediation', I am using the current jargon. German theological writing throws around the word 'mediation' (*Vermittlung*), together with its cognate words, very freely, and it has become common in English and French writings influenced by German thought. In general usage the word is vague, indicating the function of what comes in between, what forms a connecting link between two terms, intervening to relate them in some way. Behind its present currency lies its use by Hegel. According to Hegel's system, things do not exist on their own, that is 'immediately', but in relation to something else and ultimately in relation to the whole, that is 'mediately'. Further, in Hegel's dialectic, things emerge by overcoming their opposites. Hence any development comes from two opposed but linked principles. To say, then, that theology is faith mediated by some cultural element is to see theology as produced by the active relationship of faith and culture, with the suggestion of some opposition between those two principles.

4 Bauer (1976: 215) in agreement with Metz himself in conversation claims that Metz was the first to introduce the term 'orthopraxis' into theological discussion. (See Metz, 1965a: 233, 241.) That may be true of the discussion in Catholic theology or even in political theology generally. But the Greek Orthodox theologian, Nissiotis, already uses 'orthopraxia' in an article in *The Ecumenical Review* for 1961 (Nissiotis, 26–7). I owe this reference to Philip Hefner.

5 When I was writing this book, preparations were being made for the Third General Conference of Latin American Bishops at Puebla, Mexico, to be held in October 1978 (CELAM III). The fear was that this would undo the achievement of Medellín. There were grounds for that fear. Quite a number of the bishops had since Medellín already drawn back from its implications because of second thoughts about the extent of the changes it demanded and because of pressure from the national oligarchies and their international overlords. There was also a concerted campaign to bring about a reversal of Medellín in Puebla. The Preliminary Document or

official working paper distributed to the bishops for the Puebla meeting had been prepared secretly without the collaboration of the major Latin American theologians. It represented a rejection of the approach of the theology of liberation in favour of the establishment of a new Christendom (MacEoin, 1978a and 1978b). As is known, the Conference was postponed to the following year because of the death of Pope Paul VI. When it was finally held under Pope John Paul II, its results, like those of the Pope's personal visit to Mexico, were ambiguous. The worst fears of the supporters of the theology of liberation were not realized, but because of the uncertain meaning of much that was done and said, it is too early to assess the Conference in all its implications and possible consequences.

6 I have borrowed the epithet 'original' from Hegel's account of the varieties of historical writing, where 'original history' is history written by those who have themselves lived through the events they describe (Hegel, 1975b: 12).

7 Schillebeeckx (1974: 102–55) has already discussed the question of a critical theology in relation to the critical theory of society, especially as that is represented in the writings of Habermas. Schillebeeckx's particular interest is in the contribution of criticism to theological hermeneutics. While his account has some valuable insights, for which I am grateful, it precedes Habermas's recent work on the theory of communication and therefore does not meet the present state of the questions as discussed in this book, especially in chapter 4.

8 The reference, which will not escape American readers, is to Horatio Alger Jr. (1832–99), a prolific writer of popular stories for boys, all of which developed the theme that to struggle with honesty against poverty, resisting temptation, always resulted in wealth and success. Millions of copies of his books were sold.

9 See Moltmann's 'Die Kategorie *Novum* in der christlichen Theologie' in the *Festschrift, Ernst Bloch zu Ehren*, hrsg. von Siegfried Unseld (Frankfurt: Suhrkamp, 1965), 243–63. There is a more popular treatment of the same theme in Jürgen Moltmann, *Religion, Revolution, and the Future* (New York: Scribner's, 1969), 3–18. Metz also contributed to the Bloch *Festschrift*. See his 'Gott vor uns: Statt eines theologischen Arguments', *ibid.*, 117–241.

10 The interpretation and reconstruction of historical materialism is a constant theme in the works of Habermas, but a brief statement of Marxism as a philosophy of history with a practical intent is found in *Theorie und Praxis: Sozialphilosophische Studien*, Vierte durchgesehene, erweiterte und neu eingeleitete Auflage. (Frankfurt: Suhrkamp, 1972.) The relevant essay is not given in the English edition, *Theory and Practice*, London: Heinemann, 1974.

11 But for Richardson, 'ideology' has a decidedly pejorative sense. It is theoretical totalism, having bureaucracy or practical totalism as its counterpart. Ideology presupposes that society is not composed of a plurality of separate and incommensurate interests, but is a single system. Ideologies suppress the contradictions in existing society, pretending that the goals, values and interests of everyone can be brought under a single world-view. Granted that Segundo uses 'ideology' in the good or at least neutral sense of any particular system of goals and means, I wonder whether the awareness he shows of the succession of ideologies in time is accompanied by a similar awareness of the need to allow a simultaneous plurality of ideologies in his sense. His absolutizing of the Christian tradition as an educational process raises the question how Christians, if they thus adhere

absolutely to the process of their own tradition, can enter into a genuine political community with people of other traditions.

12 A further complication is the special relation of the emancipatory interest to self-reflection. The emancipatory interest becomes actual as a conscious orientation in the knowledge given in self-reflection, which frees consciousness from unrecognized dependencies and thus fulfils that interest. 'I *experience* the compulsion', Habermas writes, 'stemming from unanalyzed (but self-produced) objectivations only at the point where I become analytically conscious of, and try to *dissolve*, this pseudo-objectivity which is rooted in unconscious motives or repressed interests' (1973a: 176 – Habermas's italics). That indeed sounds very idealist, because it seems to equate emancipation with the knowledge given in self-reflection. But this impression of idealism is offset by other aspects of Habermas's work. He acknowledges that the process of enlightenment through self-reflection depends for its possibility and extent upon social and political conditions (1970a: 24–44). Again, self-reflection takes, as I said in the last chapter, the form of an explanatory understanding, dependent upon and applying a critical theory, which itself is empirically based. Self-reflection, therefore, remains closely bound up with concrete social reality and the scientific knowledge of it.

13 Habermas outlines three differences between critique and reconstruction. First, critique deals with pseudo-objects, pseudo-nature, illusion; reconstruction with objective data consciously created by the subject, such as sentences or actions. Second, critique deals with what is particular, the specific course of self-formation of an individual subject or group; reconstruction with anonymous rule systems that can be followed by any subject with the relevant competence. Third, critique makes conscious what has previously been unconscious and does so in a manner having practical consequence; reconstruction makes explicit the implicit knowledge we have when we have competence with respect to rules, but the theoretical knowledge it thus gives has of itself no practical consequences.

14 Habermas writes: 'The status of a theory designed for enlightenment entails the distinctive characteristic that its claim to truth must be tested on various levels. The first step of corroboration is scientific discourse: there the claim to truth of theoretically derived hypotheses is supported or refuted in the usual form of scientific argumentation. Naturally a theory which does not survive discursive examination must be rejected, and, of course, the claim to validity of reflexive theories can only be confirmed tentatively. But it can only be realized in the successful processes of enlightenment, which lead to the acceptance by those concerned, free of any compulsion, of the theoretically derivable interpretations. To be sure, processes of enlightenment, too, merely support the theory's claim to truth, without validating it, as long as all those potentially involved, to whom the theoretical interpretation has reference, have not had the chance of accepting or rejecting the interpretation offered *under suitable circumstances*' (1974a: 37–8 – Habermas's italics). But what precisely can be validated by the acceptance of those concerned? I suggest that interpretations are validated by the acceptance of those concerned only in so far as they refer to and are confirmed by data immediately accessible to the persons involved. Individual psychoanalytic interpretation is confirmed in that way. The person is able to confirm the validity of the interpretation in his own subjective reality and remembered personal history. The interpretation of an actual social situation may likewise be recognized as valid by reference to the

experienced data. In that way, for example, women are being led to recognize their present oppression. But when a critical theory interprets data not immediately accessible, but requiring research and ordering, as in theories concerning the structure of late capitalist society, the origin of the family, of private property or of the State, any liberating effects of such theories upon people cannot be said to offer much confirmation to their theoretical claims.

15 The debate was opened by Habermas's review of *Wahrheit und Methode* in his 'Zur Logik der Sozialwissenschaften', *Philosophische Rundschau*, Beiheft 5 (Tübingen: Mohr & Siebeck, 1967), 149–76. This and the subsequent pieces in the debate have been gathered together in *Hermeneutik und Ideologiekritik* (Frankfurt: Suhrkamp, 1971). Paul Ricoeur has a commentary on the debate, 'Herméneutique et critique des idéologies' in *Démythisation et Idéologie. Actes du Colloque organisé par le Centre International d'Etudes Humanistes et par l'Institut d'Etudes philosophiques de Rome, 4–9 Janvier, 1973* (Aubier: Éditions Montaigne, 1973).

16 For a summary account of the Frankfurt School's criticism of Marx, see the Introduction by Thomas McCarthy in Jürgen Habermas, *Legitimation Crisis* (London: Heinemann, 1976). For a more detailed account and discussion, see Albrecht Wellmer, *Critical Theory of Society* (New York: Seabury, 1974).

17 The passage is from *Kritische Theorie*, 1968, I, 198. I quote the passage as translated in Lenhardt's article (1975: 140).

18 Scholes and Kellogg place narrative in relation to other forms of literary expression: 'By narrative we mean all those literary works which are distinguished by two characteristics: the presence of a story and a story-teller. A drama is a story without a story-teller; in it characters act out directly what Aristotle called an "imitation" of such action as we find in life. A lyric, like a drama, is a direct presentation, in which a single actor, the poet or his surrogate, sings, or muses, or speaks for us to hear or to overhear. Add a second speaker . . . we move towards drama. Let the speaker tell of an event . . . and we move towards narrative. For writing to be narrative no more and no less than a teller and a tale are required' (Scholes and Kellogg, 1966: 4).

Bibliography

Adorno, Theodore W. 1973. *Negative Dialectics*. New York: Seabury.
Adorno, Theodore W. *et al.* 1976. *The Positivist Dispute in German Sociology*. London: Heinemann.
Aristotle. 1966. *The Ethics of Aristotle: The Nicomachean Ethics*. Trans. by J. A. K. Thomson. Harmondsworth: Penguin.
Augustine, Saint. 1848. *Expositions on the Book of Psalms*, vol. II, A Library of the Fathers. Oxford.
1943. *Confessions*. Trans. by J. F. Sheed. London: Sheed & Ward.
Barnes, Barry. 1977. *Interests and the Growth of Knowledge*. London: Routledge & Kegan Paul.
Bateson, Gregory. 1972. *Steps to an Ecology of Mind*. New York: Ballantine.
Bauer, Gerhard. 1976. *Christliche Hoffnung und menschlicher Fortschritt: Die politische Theologie von J. B. Metz als theologische Begründung gesellschaftlicher Verantwortung des Christen*. Mainz: Grünewald.
Benjamin, Walter. 1973. *Illuminations*. Edited and with an Introduction by Hannah Arendt. Glasgow: Fontana/Collins.
Bernstein, Richard J. 1976. *The Restructuring of Social and Political Theory*. Oxford: Blackwell.
Böhler, Dietrich. 1970a. 'Kritische Theorie – kritisch reflektiert'. *Archiv für Rechts- u. Sozialphilosophie*, 56, Heft 4, 511–25.
1970b. 'Das Problem des "emanzipatorischen Interesses" und seine gesellschaftliche Wahrnehmung'. *Zeitschrift für Evangelisches Ethik*, 14, pp. 220–40.
Brazill, William J. 1970. *The Young Hegelians*. New Haven: Yale University Press.
Burke, T. Patrick, ed. 1966. *The Word in History: The St. Xavier Symposium*. New York: Sheed & Ward.
Christensen, Darrel E., ed. 1970. *Hegel and the Philosophy of Religion: The Wofford Symposium*. The Hague: Nijhoff.
Cobb, John B. Jr., and Hodgson, Peter C. 1977. 'Wolfhart Pannenberg, "Theology and the Philosophy of Science"'. *Religious Studies Review*, 3, pp. 213–18.
Colletti, Lucio, ed. 1975. *Karl Marx: Early Writings*. Harmondsworth:

Penguin.

Comstock, Richard. 1976. 'The Marxist critique of religion: a persisting ambiguity'. *Journal of the American Academy of Religion*, XLIV, June, 327–44.

Cone, James H. 1970. *A Black Theology of Liberation*. New York: Lippincott.

Cox, Harvey. 1965. *The Secular City*. New York: Macmillan.

Crossan, John Dominic. 1975. *The Dark Interval: Towards a Theology of Story*. Niles, Illinois: Argus Communications.

Daly, Mary. 1973. *Beyond God the Father: Toward a Philosophy of Women's Liberation*. Boston: Beacon.

Davis, Charles. 1973. 'Theology and praxis'. *Cross Currents*, Summer, 154–68.

   1974. 'The philosophical foundations of pluralism' in *Le pluralisme: Symposium interdisciplinaire/Pluralism: Its Meaning Today*. Montreal: Fides.

   1976. *Body as Spirit: The Nature of Religious Feeling*. New York: Seabury.

Döbert, Rainer. 1973. *Systemtheorie und die Entwicklung religiöser Deutungssysteme: Zur Logik des sozialwissenschaftlichen Funktionalismus*. Frankfurt: Suhrkamp.

Fackenheim, Emil L. 1967. *The Religious Dimension in Hegel's Thought*. Bloomington, Ind.: Indiana University Press.

Fierro, Alfredo. 1977. *The Militant Gospel: An Analysis of Contemporary Political Theologies*. London: SCM.

Fiorenza, Francis P. 1975. 'Political theology and liberation theology: an inquiry into their fundamental meaning' in Thomas M. McFadden, ed. *Liberation, Revolution, and Freedom: Theological Perspectives*. New York: Seabury, 3–29.

Frostin, Per. 1978. *Materialismus, eine Ideologie, Religion: die materialistische Religionskritik bei Karl Marx*. München: Kaiser.

Gadamer, Hans-Georg. 1975. *Truth and Method*. London: Sheed & Ward.

Gay, Peter. 1966. *The Enlightenment: An Interpretation. The Rise of Modern Paganism*. London: Weidenfeld and Nicolson.

Gogarten, Friedrich. 1970. *Despair and Hope For Our Time*. Philadelphia/Boston: Pilgrim Press.

Gouldner, Alvin W. 1976. *The Dialectic of Ideology and Technology: The Origins, Grammar, and Future of Ideology*. New York: MacMillan.

Gutiérrez, Gustave. 1973. *A Theology of Liberation: History, Politics and Salvation*. Maryknoll, New York: Orbis.

Habermas, Jürgen. 1962. *Strukturwandel der Öffentlichkeit: Untersuchungen zu einer Kategorie der bürgerlichen Gesellschaft*. Neuwied und Berlin: Luchterhand.

   1967. Zur Logik der Sozialwissenschaften in *Philosophische Runds-*

chau, hrsg. von Hans-Georg Gadamer und Helmut Kuhn, Beiheft 5. Tübingen: J. C. B. Mohr (Paul Siebeck).

1970a. 'Bedingungen für eine Revolutionierung spätkapitalistischer Gesellschaftssysteme' in *Marx und die Revolution*. Vorträge von Ernst Bloch, Herbert Marcuse, Jürgen Habermas *et al.* Frankfurt: Suhrkamp.

1970b. 'Der Universalitätsanspruch der Hermeneutik' in *Hermeneutik und Ideologiekritik*. Frankfurt: Suhrkamp, 1971, 120–59.

1971a. *Philosophisch–politische Profile*. Frankfurt: Suhrkamp.

1971b. 'Vorbereitende Bemerkungen zu einer Theorie der kommunikativen Kompetenz' in Habermas, Jürgen and Luhmann, Niklas, *Theorie der Gesellschaft der Sozialtechnologie–Was leistet die Systemforschung*. Frankfurt: Suhrkamp, 101–41.

1971c. *Toward a Rational Society*. London: Heinemann.

1972a. *Theorie und Praxis: Sozialphilosophische Studien*. Vierte durchgesehene erweiterte und neu eingeleitete Auflage.

1972b. *Knowledge and Human Interests*. Trans. by Jeremy J. Shapiro. Boston: Beacon Press.

1973a. 'A postscript to knowledge and human interests'. *Philosophy of the Social Sciences*, 3, pp. 157–89.

1973b. 'Wahrheitstheorien' in *Wirklichkeit und Reflexion: Festschrift für Walter Schulz*. Pfullingen: Neske, 211–65.

1974a. *Theory and Practice*. London: Heinemann.

1974b. 'On Social Identity'. *Telos*, no. 19 (Spring), 91–103.

1975. *Erkenntnis und Interesse mit einem neuen Nachwort*. Frankfurt: Suhrkamp. For an English translation of the Postscript, see *Philosophy of the Social Sciences*, 3 (1973), 157–89.

1976a. *Legitimation Crisis*. London: Heinemann.

1976b. *Zur Rekonstruktion des Historischen Materialismus*. Frankfurt: Suhrkamp.

1976c. 'Some Distinctions in Universal Pragmatics: A Working Paper'. *Theory and Society*, 3, pp. 155–67.

1977. 'Aspects of the rationality of action'. Paper given at Conference on Rationality Today at the University of Ottawa, 27–30 Oct. 1977. Published in Theodore F. Geraets, ed., *Rationality Today/La Rationalité aujourd'hui* (Ottawa: Editions de l'Université d'Ottowa/The University of Ottowa Press, 1979), 185-205.

Habermas, Jürgen and Heinrich, Dieter. 1974. *Zwei Reden*. Frankfurt: Suhrkamp.

Habermas, Jürgen and Luhmann, Niklas. 1971. *Theorie der Gesellschaft der Sozialtechnologie – Was leistet die Systemforschung*. Frankfurt: Suhrkamp.

Hales, E. E. Y. 1965. *Pope John and His Revolution*. London: Eyre & Spottiswode.

Harris, H. S. 1972. *Hegel's Development: Toward the Sunlight 1770–1801*.

Bibliography

Oxford: Clarendon Press.

Hazard, Paul. 1973. *The European Mind 1680–1715*. Trans. by J. Lewis May. Penguin University Books edn. Harmondsworth: Penguin.

Heer, Friedrich. 1966. *The Intellectual History of Europe*. London: Weidenfeld and Nicolson.

Hegel, G. W. F. 1968. *Gesammelte Werke*, 4: *Jenaer Kritische Schriften*, hrsg. von Hartmut Buchner und Otto Pöggeler. Hamburg: Meiner.

1975a, *Hegel's Logic: Being – Part One of the Encyclopaedia of the Philosophical Sciences (1830)*. Trans. by William Wallace. Oxford: Clarendon Press.

1975b. *Lectures on the Philosophy of World History: Introduction: Reason in History*. Trans. by H. B. Nisbet. Cambridge: Cambridge University Press.

1975c. *Phänomenologie des Geistes*. Suhrkamp Taschenbuch, Wissenschaft 8. Frankfurt: Suhrkamp.

Hennelly, Alfred T. 1977. 'The challenge of Juan Luis Segundo'. *Theological Studies*, 38, pp. 125—35.

Hermeneutik und Ideologiekritik. 1971. Frankfurt: Suhrkamp.

Hesse, Mary. 1972. 'In defence of objectivity'. *Proceedings of the British Academy*, vol. 58. London: Oxford University Press, 275–92.

Horkheimer, Max. 1968. *Kritische Theorie*. 2 Bde. Frankfurt: Fischer.

1972. *Critical Theory: Selected Essays*. Trans. by Matthew J. O'Connel and others. New York: Herder & Herder.

1974.[2] *Eclipse of Reason*. New York: Seabury.

1975. *Die Sehnsucht nach dem ganz Anderen: Ein Interview mit Kommentar von Helmut Gumnior*. Hamburg: Furche.

Horkheimer, Max and Adorno, Theodore W. 1972. *Dialectic of Enlightenment*. New York: Seabury.

Jay, Martin. 1973. *The Dialectical Imagination: A History of the Frankfurt School and the Institute of Social Research 1923–1950*. Boston/Toronto: Little Brown.

Johns, Roger Duk. 1976. *Man in the World: The Political Theology of Johannes Baptist Metz*. American Academy of Religion: Dissertation Series, no. 16. Missoula, Montana: Scholars Press.

Kant, Immanuel. 1965. *Critique of Pure Reason*. Trans. by Norman Kemp Smith. New York: St. Martin's Press.

Koselleck, Reinhart. 1959. *Kritik und Krise: Ein Beitrag zur Pathogenese der bürgerlichen Welt*. Orbis Academicus. Freiburg/München: Karl Alber.

Lavalette, Henri de. 1970. 'La "théologie politique" de Jean-Baptiste Metz'. *Recherches de Sciences Religieuses*, 58, pp. 321–50.

Leeuwen, Arend Th. Van. 1972. *Critique of Heaven: The first series of the Gifford Lectures entitled 'Critique of Heaven and Earth'*. London: Lutterworth.

Lenhardt, Christian. 1975. 'Anamnestic solidarity: the proletariat and its *Manes*'. *Telos*, no. 25, Fall.

Lonergan, Bernard. 1958. *Insight: A Study of Human Understanding*. London: Longmans, Green.

1974. *A Second Collection: Papers by Bernard J.F. Lonergan*. Ed. by William F. J. Ryan and Bernard J. Tyrrell. London: Darton, Longman & Todd.

McCarthy, T. A. 1976. 'A theory of communicative competence' in Paul Connerton, ed., *Critical Sociology: Selected Readings*. Harmondsworth: Penguin.

MacEoin, Gary, ed. 1978a. *Puebla: Moment of Decision for the Latin American Church*: Special Issue of *Cross Currents*, XXVIII, no. 1 (Spring).

1978b. 'The Stakes at CELAM III'. *Commonweal*, CV, 495–8.

McLellan, David. 1973. *Karl Marx: His Life and Thought*. London: Macmillan.

Macpherson, C. B. 1975. *The Political Theory of Possessive Individualism: Hobbes to Locke*. Oxford: Oxford University Press.

Mann, Peter, O.S.B. 1969–70. 'The transcendental or the political kingdom: reflexions on a theological dispute'. *New Blackfriars*, L (1969), 805–12; LI (1970), 4–16.

Marcuse, Herbert. 1964. *One-Dimensional Man: Studies in the Ideology of Advanced Industrial Society*. Boston: Beacon Press.

Maritain, Jacques. 1973. *Integral Humanism: Temporal and Spiritual Problems of a New Christendom*. Trans. by Joseph W. Evans. Notre Dame, Indiana: University of Notre Dame Press.

Martin, David. 1969. *The Religious and the Secular*. London: Routledge & Kegan Paul.

Marx, Karl. 1946. *Capital*. 2 vols. Everyman's Library. London: Deutsch. New York: Dutton.

Massanari, Ronald. 1977. 'The politics of imagination: playful theologies as theologies of imagination'. *Cross Currents*, XXVII, 199–204.

May, John R. 1976. *The Pruning Word: The Parables of Flannery O'Connor*. Notre Dame & London: University of Notre Dame Press.

Meeks, M. Douglas. 1974. *Origins of the Theology of Hope*. Philadelphia: Fortress.

Metz, Johann Baptist. 1960. 'The responsibility of hope'. *Philosophy Today*, X, 4 (Winter, 1966).

1962. *Christliche Anthropozentrik: Über die Denkform des Thomas von Aquin*. München: Kösel.

1965a. 'Gott vor uns: Statt eines theologischen Arguments' in *Ernst Bloch zu Ehren: Beiträge zu seinem Werk*, hrsg. von S. Unseld.

Frankfurt: Suhrkamp, 227–41.

1965b. 'Unbelief as a theological problem'. *Concilium*, 6, pp. 59–77.

1969a. *Reform und Gegenreformation heute*. Mainz: Grünewald.

1969b. '"Politische Theologie" in der Diskussion' in *Diskussion zur 'politischen Theologie'*, hrsg. von Helmut Peukert. München: Kaiser/Mainz: Grünewald, 267–301.

1970a. 'Political theology' in *Sacramentum Mundi: An Encyclopaedia of Theology*. Vol. 5. London: Burns Oates.

1970b. *Befreiendes Gedächtnis Jesu Christi*. Mainz: Grünewald.

1972a. 'The future *Ex Memoria Passionis*' in Ewert H. Cousins, ed., *Hope and the Future of Man*, Philadelphia: Fortress Press, 117–131.

1972b. 'Grond en functie van de politieke theologie'. *Tijdschrift voor Theologie*, 12, pp. 159–70.

1973a. *Theology of the World*. New York: Seabury.

1973b. 'Erinnerung'. *Handbuch philosophischer Grundbegriffe*, I, München, 386–96.

1973c. 'A short apology of narrative'. *Concilium*. N.S., vol. 5, no. 9, 84–96.

1974. 'Kirche und Volk; oder der Preis der Orthodoxie'. *Stimmen der Zeit*, 192, pp. 797–811.

1977a. *Glaube in Geschichte und Gesellschaft: Studien zu einer praktischen Fundamentaltheologie*. Mainz: Grünewald.

1977b. *Zeit der Orden? Zur Mystik und Politik der Nachfolge*. Freiburg/Basel/Wien: Herder.

Metz, Johann Baptist, Moltmann, Jürgen, Oelmüller, Willi. 1970. *Kirche im Prozess der Aufklärung: Aspekte einer neuen 'politischen Theologie'. Gesellschaft und Theologie. Systematische Beiträge*. No. 1. München: Kaiser/Mainz: Grünewald.

Mojzes, Paul, ed. 1978. *Varieties of Christian–Marxist Dialogue*. Philadelphia: Ecumenical Press.

Moltmann, Jürgen. 1964. *Theologie der Hoffnung*. München: Kaiser.

1967. *Theology of Hope*. New York: Harper.

1969. *Religion, Revolution and the Future*. New York: Scribners.

1970. 'Theologische Kritik der politischen Religion' in J. B. Metz, J. Moltmann, W. Oelmüller, *Kirche im Prozess der Aufklärung: Aspekte einer neuen 'politischen Theologie'. Gesellschaft und Theologie, Systematische Beiträge*. No. 1. München: Kaiser/Mainz: Grünewald, 11–51. Eng. trans. in J. Moltmann *et al.*, *Religion and Political Society*. New York: Harper, 1974, 9–47.

1975. *The Experiment Hope*. Ed. and trans. with a Foreword by M. Douglas Meeks. Philadelphia: Fortress Press.

Murray, John Courtney. 1954. 'The problem of pluralism in America'. *Thought*, 29.

1960. *We Hold These Truths: Catholic Reflections on the American Proposition*. New York: Sheed & Ward.

Nissiotis, N. A. 1961. 'Interpreting orthodoxy'. *The Ecumenical Review*, 14 (1961–2), 3–28.

O'Connor, Flannery. 1969. *Mystery and Manners*. New York: Farrar, Straus and Giroux.

O'Neill, John, ed. 1976. *On Critical Theory*. London: Heinemann.

Oudenrijn, Frans van den. 1972. *Kritische Theologie als Kritik der Theologie: Theorie und Praxis bei Karl Marx – Herausforderung der Theologie. Gesellschaft und Theologie, Systematische Beiträge* 8. München: Kaiser/Mainz: Grünewald.

Padover, Saul K. 1978. *Karl Marx: An Intimate Biography*. New York: McGraw-Hill.

Pannenberg, Wolfhart. 1963. 'Hermeneutik und Universalgeschichte'. *Zeitschrift für Theologie und Kirche*, 60, pp. 90–121.

1973. *Wissenschaftstheorie und Theologie*. Frankfurt: Suhrkamp.

1976. *Theology and the Philosophy of Science*. Philadelphia: Westminster.

Peukert, Helmut, Hrsg. 1969. *Diskussion zur 'politischen Theologie'*. München: Kaiser/Mainz: Grünewald.

1976. *Wissenschaftstheorie – Handlungstheorie – fundamentale Theologie. Analysen zu Ansatz und Status theologischer Theoriebildung*. Düsseldorf: Patmos.

Prufer, Thomas. 1963. 'A protreptic: what is philosophy?' in *Studies in Philosophy and the History of Philosophy*, II. Washington.

Ramsey, Ian T. 1957. *Religious Language*. New York: Macmillan.

Religion and Political Society. 1974. Jürgen Moltmann, Herbert W. Richardson, Johann Baptist Metz, Willi Oelmüller, M. Darrol Bryant. Ed. and trans. by The Institute of Christian Thought. Harper: New York.

Rendtorff, Trutz. 1969. *Christentum ausserhalb der Kirche: Konkretionen der Aufklärung*. Hamburg: Furche.

Ricoeur, Paul. 1973. 'Herméneutique et critique des idéologies' in *Démythisation et idéologie: Actes du Colloque organisé par le Centre International d'Etudes Humanistes et par l'Institut d'Etudes philosophique de Rome*, 4–9 janvier. Enrico Castelli, ed. (Aubier: Ed. Montaigne, 1973), 25–61.

1974. 'Philosophy and religious language'. *The Journal of Religion*, Jan., 71–85.

1975. 'Biblical hermeneutics'. *Semeia*, 4, pp. 29–148.

Schaeffer, H. 1972. '"Politicke Theologie" in een tijd van "religieuze renaissance"'. *Tijdschrift voor Theologie*, 12, pp. 225–43.

Schall, James V. 1977. 'Catholicism and intelligence: the reconciliation of the world and truth'. *The Clergy Review*, 62, pp. 258–65.

Schillebeeckx, Edward. 1974. *The Understanding of Faith: Interpretation and Criticism*. A Crossroad Book. New York: Seabury Press.

Scholes, Robert and Kellogg, Robert. 1966. *The Nature of Narrative*.

New York: Oxford University Press.

Segundo, Juan Luis. 1977. *The Liberation of Theology*. Dublin: Gill and Macmillan.

Shiner, Larry. 1966. *The Secularization of History: An Introduction to the Theology of Friedrich Gogarten*. Nashville: Abingdon.

1967. 'The concept of secularization in empirical research'. *Journal for the Scientific Study of Religion*, 6, pp. 207–20.

Shook, L. K., ed. 1968. *Theology of Renewal: Proceedings of the Congress on the Theology of the Renewal of the Church Centenary of Canada, 1867–1967*. 2 vols. Montreal: Palm.

Siebert, Rudolf. 1974. 'Religion in the perspective of critical sociology'. *Concilium*, N.S., vol. 1, no. 10, Jan., 56–69.

1976a. 'Max Horkheimer: theology and positivism I'. *The Ecumenist*, 14, no. 2 (Jan.–Feb.), 19–24.

1976b. 'Max Horkheimer: theology and positivism II'. *The Ecumenist*, 14, no. 3 (Mar.–Apr.), 42–5.

1976c. 'Horkheimer's sociology of religion'. *Telos*, no. 30 (Winter 1976–7), 127–44.

Smith, Donald Eugene. 1970. *Religion and Political Development*. The Little Brown Series in Comparative Politics. Boston: Little Brown.

Smith, Wilfred Cantwell. 1976. *Religious Diversity: Essays*. Ed. by Willard G. Oxtoby. A Harper Forum Book. New York: Harper.

1977. 'Interpreting religious interrelations: an historian's view of Christian and Muslim'. *SR: Studies in Religion/Sciences Religieuses*, vol. 6, no. 5 (1976–7), 515–26.

Sölle, Dorothee. 1974. *Political Theology*. Trans. and with an Introduction by John Shelley. Philadelphia: Fortress Press.

Southern, R. W. 1970. *Western Society and the Church in the Middle Ages*. The Pelican History of the Church. Harmondsworth: Penguin.

Taylor, Charles. 1971. 'Interpretation and the sciences of man'. *Review of Metaphysics*, 25, pp. 3–51.

1975. *Hegel*. Cambridge: Cambridge University Press.

Unseld, Siegfried, Hrsg. 1965. *Ernst Bloch zu Ehren*. Frankfurt: Suhrkamp.

Wellmer, Albrecht. 1974. *Critical Theory of Society*. A Continuum Book. New York: Seabury.

Wiedenhofer, Siegfried. 1976. *Politische Theologie*. Stuttgart: Kohlhammer.

Xhaufflaire, Marcel. 1972. *La 'Théologie politique': Introduction à la théologie politique de J. B. Metz*. Tome I. Paris: Editions du Cerf.

Xhaufflaire, Marcel and Derksen, K. 1970. *Les deux visages de la théologie de la sécularisation: Analyse critique de la théologie de la sécularisation*. Tournai: Casterman.

Index

action and discourse, 87–9, 92–3, 102
Adorno, Theodore W., 83, 134, 137, 138
anamnestic solidarity, 144–5
Aquinas, Thomas, 44
Aristotle, 21
Assman, Hugo, 60
Augustine, Saint, 158

Bateson, Gregory, 55
Bayle, Pierre, 106
Benjamin, Walter, 141–3
black theology, 11
Bloch, Ernst, 30
Bossuet, 106

Christian faith, 66–7; as critique, 73–4
Christian tradition, 8, 9, 57; source of political theories, policy and action, 65–9
Church: and society, 32–4; and political action, 74
classicist mentality, 1, 182 n.1
communicative action, 81–2, 92–3; and death, 146–9
Cone, James, 11, 12, 52
critical theology, 24–5, 73–4, 104
critical theory, 71–2, 87, 184 n.14; see also Frankfurt School
critical tradition, see critique
criticism, see critique
critique: and Habermas, 84–7; and Hegel, 109–14; and Marx, 115–17; and reconstruction, 85–6, 184 n.13; and the Absolute State, 107–8; and the bourgeoisie, 108–9; and the Frankfurt School, 117–19; history of, 105–19; c. of ideology, 7, 71, 87; c. of religion, 119–32; use of word, 104–5

Daly, Mary, 10–11

deprivatization, 15, 175, 177
discourse, see action and discourse

emancipation: and self-reflection, 184 n.12; interest in, 70–1; rational grounding of, 95–7

feminist theology, 10–11
Feuerbach, Ludwig, 124–5
Fierro, Alfredo, 10, 61, 63
Frankfurt School, 22–3, 78, 117–19, 132
freedom: and tradition, 102–3, 149–50; modern history of, 46–9

Gadamer, Hans-Georg, 83, 97–8
Gogarten, Friedrich, 36–43

Habermas, Jürgen, 21, 77–103, 145, 179; and Gadamer, 83–4, 97–9; action and discourse, 87–9; analysis of capitalist society, 40–3; communication theory of society, 94–5; communicative action, 81–2, 92–3; critique, 84–7; emancipation, rational grounding of, 95–7; ideal speech situation, 93–4; knowledge and human interests, 69–72; political action, 72; problem of identity, 163–6; rejection of positivism, 80; religion, 138–42; social evolution, 159–63; tradition, 97–9; universal pragmatics, 91–2
Hegel, 104, 109–14, 120–3, 164–5, 174
hermeneutics: and communicative action, 82; and science, 100–1; and tradition, 98–9
Horkheimer, Max, 18, 78–9, 83, 117, 118, 133, 140; exchange with Benjamin about history, 142–3; on religion, 134–8

195

196